STUDIES IN MILTON

Dr. Tillyard's book comprises ten essays, of which the majority are concerned with the epic poems; others discuss *Comus* and Milton's non-poetic works. The most considerable and perhaps the most controversial paper that is entitled *The Crisis of Paradise Lost*, in which Dr. Tillyard advances a new theory as to the point of climax in the poem; this entails a change of balance affecting the whole conception of Milton's design, and especially the much disputed importance of Satan's role.

Dr. Tillyard's pre-eminence as a Miltonic scholar, coupled with his gift for lucid exposition, assures the value of *Studies in Milton* for the specialist and the general reader alike.

Studies in

MILTON

★

E. M. W. Tillyard

CEDRIC CHIVERS LTD
PORTWAY
BATH

First published 1951
by
Chatto & Windus Ltd
This edition published
by
Cedric Chivers Ltd
by arrangement with the copyright holder
at the request of
The London & Home Counties Branch
of
The Library Association
1973

SBN 85594 899 X

821.4
TIL

Printed in Great Britain by
Redwood Press Limited, Trowbridge, Wiltshire
Bound by Cedric Chivers Ltd, Bath

Contents

NOTE

Quotations from Milton's prose works (except the Letters and Academic Exercises) are taken, by kind permission of the Oxford University Press, from the following volumes of *The Works of John Milton*, copyright by Columbia University Press: vol. iii (1931), vol. iv (1931), vol vi (1932).

Preface

IT is about twenty years since I wrote my *Milton*; and much has happened in Milton scholarship in the interval. It is therefore only to be expected that on some matters I should have modified my opinion. But it is no use trying to graft such modifications on a book that attempted some proportion of treatment; for that would be to spoil any value it had as a whole, including its possible interest as a period piece. There is no harm, however, in separate enlargement and correction; and these are the things that *Studies in Milton* aims largely at providing. The longest study, on the crisis of *Paradise Lost*, corrects a common assumption (to which I had yielded in my *Milton*) and in substitution advances a general interpretation of the ninth and tenth books which, if true, has important bearings on the success of the whole poem. The next longest study makes the difficult attempt to conjecture what portions of Milton's theology (about which so much has been found out in the last twenty years) passed most readily into his poetry. It supplements rather than corrects my section on Milton's beliefs in my earlier book. Many of the other studies have the same end of supplementing or correcting; and in the light, partly of recent scholarship, partly of my own maturer thought.

The bulk of recent Milton scholarship is formidable, and a proportion of it is good. It is also world-wide. For instance, between 1942 and 1947, there were published (apart from specialist studies) five books on *Paradise Lost* alone, all good in their ways and all by men born in different countries: C. S. Lewis (England), Douglas Bush (Canada), John S. Diekhoff (United States), B. Rajan (India), A. J. A. Waldock (Australia). It is typical, too, that these books (in the aggregate) treat preponderatingly of Milton's thought, and in so doing avoid the characteristic vice of the Romantic critics of Milton: that of keeping Milton's poetry and thought separate. Yet, by this very avoidance, so right in itself, they indicate a danger to which many modern critics are liable; which is to ignore, in the act of correcting the errors of the Romantic critics, the things in Milton which those critics were peculiarly fitted to perceive. To this danger E. E. Stoll has called attention in his articles on Milton's own romantic side; and we should do well to heed him.

Most of these studies are new, and are printed for the first time. The following have been printed before, and in mentioning them I wish to thank their publishers for permission to reprint. *Arnold on Milton* appeared in the *Church Quarterly Review*. The *Action of Comus* appeared in the *Essays and Studies* of the English Association and now reappears in a revised form. The *Christ of 'Paradise Regained'* appeared in *Studies in Philology*. The study of Milton's letters and prolusions was originally my introduction to Mrs P. B. Tillyard's translation of them, published by the Cambridge University Press. These Latin works of Milton are still not as well known as they deserve to be and I should be glad to help bring them before a wider public. Some of the substance of my study of Milton's theology and emotion was contained in a recent broadcast for the Third Programme.

The appendices are reprinted, by permission, the first, of *The Times Literary Supplement*, the second, of *Studies in Philology*.

When in my text I refer to Rajan and Waldock without further detail I mean B. Rajan, *Paradise Lost and the Seventeenth Century Reader* (London, 1947), and A. J. A. Waldock, *Paradise Lost and its Critics* (Cambridge, 1947), two books to which, though I have drawn upon many others, I owe a special debt.

E. M. W. T.

Arnold on Milton[1]

HOWEVER deeply we deplore the architectural destruction suffered by the City of London in the late war, we must admit a modicum of gain as well. Some slum areas were given an anticipatory clearance, and, whatever plan is chosen for laying out the ground round St Paul's, future ages will enjoy a better view of Wren's architecture than was possible before 1940. The destruction which causes us to be here today bears a mixed character. The hole torn by a bomb fragment in a window commemorating the gentle and amiable wife and the infant daughter of one of the world's great poets symbolizes sadly enough the cruel insensitiveness of total war to human virtue and to ecumenical culture; while, to turn to the smaller and more particular, the admirable energy of the Rector of St Margaret's in causing the damage to be made good represents a necessary sacrifice of energies that might have gone to create, to energies that perforce go to replace. Yet this enforced restoration of damage has its good side. It has been skilfully carried out, and it points to more than one happy event.

The original window was the gift of an American, Mr George W. Childs, of Philadelphia, of whose cordial hospitality to many Englishmen Matthew Arnold spoke. To find the money to repair the bomb damage an appeal was issued. It was answered by donations from both sides of the Atlantic. There were in 1888, when the window was dedicated, many ties of friendship existing between Great Britain and the United States of America, and Mr Childs's action of personal generosity created one of them. Today one hopes those ties are stronger; yet they are different, depending on greater mutual knowledge, a profounder critical spirit, and a measure

[1] An address delivered in St Margaret's Church, Westminster, on July 4, 1949, to commemorate the restoration of the window in memory of Milton's second wife, which had been damaged by bomb fragments in the 1939–1945 war.

1

of political co-operation which in the year 1888 would have been regarded as fabulous. In its small way this joint responsibility for making good in St Margaret's, Westminster, the damage of war represents the new approximation of the two countries.

The committee collected to sponsor the appeal included different types of religious and political opinion. In so doing it represented one of the largest changes that has occurred in England between 1888 and the present day; the drawing together of Church and Chapel. It was Matthew Arnold who delivered an address in this church when the memorial window was dedicated; and one of the ways in which to bring home to ourselves the changed relations between Church and Chapel is to read what he said about the Nonconformists. It is not that he was unfair, however critical, but that as a Churchman he spoke of an alien community. To exaggerate this drawing together would be easy; and there are still probably small towns or large villages in England where Churchmen deal with the Church grocer and Dissenters with the Chapel grocer. Nevertheless in the matter of mutual accessibility the change has been revolutionary. I believe Milton would have welcomed the change. Though he may appear to represent a doctrine of individual liberty especially dear to Nonconformity, he was a Churchman half his life. And if he inveighed against the Episcopacy, he did so—more than he realized himself—mainly for political reasons. That the social cleavage between Church and Chapel resulting from the Civil War should have lasted over two centuries he would have deplored, for he never carried his doctrinal differences into personal relations. We have only to think of his social success in Catholic Italy and of Aubrey's account of Dryden's visit to him. Dryden, the High Churchman and subsequent Catholic, sought Milton's leave to adapt the blank verse of *Paradise Lost* to his rhymed drama, *The State of Innocence*. Milton, though mildly satirical in his reply—he gave Dryden 'leave to tag his verses'—received him civilly.

But above all, the present repair of the window should indicate a renewed belief in Milton's eminence as a poet. Of that eminence Matthew Arnold, in his noble dedicatory address, had no fraction of doubt. Milton for him represented an 'ideal of high and rare excellence' which in the field of literature was the perfect antidote for that tendency to the average and the mediocre which according to Arnold is the particular crime of the Anglo-Saxon race. And his essay mainly concerns Milton's moral and stylistic elevation. Today it is fitting that I should speak briefly of some changes in men's opinion of Milton that have taken place since Arnold delivered his address here just over sixty years ago, on February 13, 1888.

'What other poet,' wrote Arnold, 'has shown so sincere a sense of the grandeur of his vocation, and a moral effort so constant and sublime to make and keep himself worthy of it?' In spite of one attempt to interpret Milton's character in terms of pride, of another in terms of Machiavellian mendacity and ruthlessness, and a third in terms of compensation for the sense of smallness set up by an inherited physical disability, the opinion still prevails that Milton was devoted to his art and that he went in awe of the solemn terms on which life is lived on this earth.

Arnold's advancement of Milton as the supreme master of the grand style in English has fared less well. For one thing, his meaning is not clear. He was taken to mean, and I think wrongly, that his long poems at any rate exhibit from first to last a style of sustained grandeur, of unremitting reverberation. Such an exhibition could only imply an intolerable strain and monotony; and Milton's verse, partly on a too easy acceptance of what Arnold can hardly have meant, has incurred that type of censure. A very little attention to the actual poetry will disprove it. The tone of many passages is moderate or even gentle. Take these lines from *Paradise Regained* spoken by Christ about the heathen philosophers:

> Alas what can they teach, and not mislead;
> Ignorant of themselves, of God much more,
> And how the world began, and how man fell
> Degraded by himself, on grace depending?
> Much of the Soul they talk, but all awrie,

> And in themselves seek vertue, and to themselves
> All glory arrogate, to God give none,
> Rather accuse him under usual names,
> Fortune and Fate, as one regardless quite
> Of mortal things.

Or take those lines of Samson in reply to his father's well-meaning attempt to comfort him that Samuel Johnson so much admired. Not only are they hushed in tone but eight out of the nine are end-stopt in flat contradiction of Milton's supposed invariable habit of sustaining his rhythms:

> All otherwise to me my thoughts portend,
> That these dark orbs no more shall treat with light,
> Nor th'other light or life continue long,
> But yield to double darkness nigh at hand:
> So much I feel my genial spirits droop,
> My hopes all flat, nature within me seems
> In all her functions weary of herself;
> My race of glory run, and race of shame,
> And I shall shortly be with them that rest.

But if Arnold meant that Milton invented a scheme of rhetoric to which he was ever loyal and which constituted a technical standard of uncommon severity then he spoke the truth and indicated a reason why between 1888 and 1949 Milton's reputation has fluctuated. Alike in conversation, in written prose, and in verse fashion moves between certain extremes of formality and informality. A well-bred young woman of the upper middle-class speaks more informally in the twentieth century than she did in Jane Austen's day; Samuel Johnson invented a more formal prose than suited Swift; the poetic diction of Donne is nearer the informality of the spoken word than is Spenser's. In spite of many cross-currents, in spite of Browning and Hardy, the late Victorian Age favoured formality. A typical good piece of expository prose like Maine's *Ancient Law* was formal and exalted in a way which would be shocking today. The most typical and influential poets, the Pre-Raphaelites, had their own very marked formalities. When, as was bound to happen, the Pre-

Raphaelite manner grew stale, the poets sought renewal through introducing the informality of the language and of the rhythms of everyday speech. Thus Yeats, in spite of his Pre-Raphaelite antecedents, can write near the end of his life in a lyric:

> 'Drown all the dogs,' said the fierce young woman,
> 'They killed my goose and a cat.
> Drown, drown in the water butt,
> Drown all the dogs,' said the fierce young woman.

And Mr Eliot near the opening of a religious poem writes

> Why should I mourn
> The vanished power of the usual reign?

where the informal word *usual* sounds fresh largely because it had lain fallow in Victorian poetry. Now Milton, though he can write quietly and can use simple words (the word *usual* occurs in the lines quoted from *Paradise Regained*), is through the order of his words always formal and rhetorical. He thus represented a stylistic tendency adverse to that of the twentieth century, and, becoming less apt to influence contemporary production, he lost some of his influence. Such loss is but temporary. In time the fashion will change again, and Milton will not only be a great classic but an inspiration to the creative writer. Indeed the change may have begun already.

Arnold's speech was brief and uncontroversial. He did not mention one matter of controversy in which recent opinion has greatly improved on the Victorian. Ever since the age of the French Revolution and Blake's assertion that Milton was on the Devil's side without knowing it, many of the ablest and most enthusiastic readers of *Paradise Lost* have made Satan its hero and centred the poem's significance in him. 'It is in Satan,' wrote Lascelles Abercrombie, 'that the imperishable significance of *Paradise Lost* is centred; his vast unyielding agony symbolizes the profound antinomy of the modern consciousness.' This opinion no longer preponderates. Scholars are now more aware of the medieval literary tradition and of how long its influence lingered, and they see that in one of its aspects *Paradise Lost* is a version of the Morality theme of Everyman, showing Adam and Eve the central figures, the hero and heroine, fought for by the powers of heaven and hell. Further, world events have forced us to study the dictator-type, which Satan so superbly represents. We now know (as we should never have forgotten) that to be greatly bad a man must have correspondingly great potentialities for good. That Milton should have depicted such potentialities in Satan argues not his covert approval but his sound knowledge of the dictator-type.

Through seeing Satan aright, we may judge better on another controversial matter which Arnold mentioned only to avoid: that is the theology or what he calls 'the inevitable matter of a Puritan epic'. Here again recent opinion has taken a better turn. Whatever weight we give to Milton's heresies, his Arianism, his beliefs that the soul died with the body and that God created the world not out of nothing but out of himself, we now see that Milton did not sympathize with Satanic pride but that, recognizing the temptation to pride in himself, he passionately embraced and expressed the ethics of Christian humility. Indeed the very structure of *Paradise Lost* is an ironic exposure of the weakness of Satanic pride (for all the reverberant protests of its power) when matched with the smallest manifestation of sincere and regenerate human feeling. Out of the apparent triumph of Satan, the eating of the apple and all the chaos that follows it, emerges the homely and miniature spectacle of two human beings coming together after their quarrel and admitting humbly their faults.

That this irony (at Satan's expense and in assertion of the doctrine of humility) is the core of *Paradise Lost* is clear from the final, recapitulatory dialogue between Adam and Michael near the end of the poem, after Michael has revealed the world's future history. When in it Adam speaks of defeating strong things by weak, we are meant to recall the grandiosities of Satan and the homeliness of Eve's reconciliation with Adam. Here is the speech:

He ended, and thus Adam last replied:
How soon hath thy prediction, seer blest,
Measur'd this transient world, the race of time,
Till time stand fixt: beyond is all abyss,
Eternity, whose end no eye can reach.
Greatly instructed I shall hence depart,
Greatly in peace of thought, and have my fill
Of knowledge, what this vessel can contain;
Beyond which was my folly to aspire.
Henceforth I learn that to obey is best,
And love with fear the only God, to walk
As in his presence, ever to observe
His providence, and on him sole depend
Merciful over all his works; with good
Still overcoming evil, and by small
Accomplishing great things, by things deem'd weak
Subverting worldly strong, and worldly wise
By simple meek: that suffering for truth's sake
Is fortitude to highest victory,
And, to the faithful, death the gate of life:
Taught this by his example whom I now
Acknowledge my redeemer ever blest.

Though so soberly spoken there is as much passion in these words as in Satan's better known defiances in the first book. And if we give these words their weight we may hope in some ways for a better understanding of *Paradise Lost* than was possible when Matthew Arnold gave his memorable address in this church.

The Crisis of Paradise Lost

IT was Walter Raleigh who spoke of the crisis of *Paradise Lost* in the tone of greatest assurance. After setting forth the vast range of topics comprised in the poem he went on:

> All these are exhibited in the clearest and most inevitable relation with the main event, so that there is not an incident, hardly a line of the poem, but leads backwards or forwards to those central lines in the Ninth Book:
>
> > So saying, her rash hand in evil hour
> > Forth-reaching to the fruit, she plucked, she eat.
> > Earth felt the wound, and Nature from her seat,
> > Sighing through all her works, gave signs of woe
> > That all was lost.
>
> From this point radiates a plot so immense in scope, that the history of the world from the first preaching of the gospel to the Millennium occupies only some fifty lines of Milton's epilogue.

And Raleigh's assurance has been compelling. When studying *Paradise Lost* for my *Milton* I accepted his statement as axiomatic; and this seems to have been a common experience. Hanford, for instance, in *A Milton Handbook*, describing how the poem evolves, assumes Book Ten to be of less moment than Book Nine, an appendage in subservience to it. Grierson in his *Milton and Wordsworth* assumes the same:

> If there is a falling off of interest in the later books it was inherent in the subject. Who could make an heroic poem of Adam and Eve tempted to transgress a tabu? Milton has done his best in the ninth book, the varied decorative material of which is all that it should be. But it is not until the Fall is accomplished that the two characters grow human and winning.

Note how Grierson assumes that the one place where there *should* be heroic action is the story of eating the fruit: for Adam and Eve to grow interesting after the Fall is to do so too late;

the idea that it is then that they find scope in noble doings simply does not arise.[1]

Now if you go to the bare story and seek a point from which all events radiate you can hardly choose otherwise than Raleigh. It might indeed be argued that the first entrance of pride into the heart of Lucifer was even more significant than the eating of the fruit, since without Lucifer's defection there would have been no gap in heaven, no need to find recruits for it from a second creation; in fact no world and no world history. And as a subject for a Miracle Play, where no elaboration of incident or of motivation is required, it does well enough. We cannot ask for better than Lucifer's unmotivated boastings at the beginning of the Towneley Cycle:

> For I am lord of blis
> Over all the world, I wis,
> My myrth is moot of all;
> Therefor my will is this,
> Master ye shall me call.

> And ye shall see full soon onone
> How that me semys to sit in trone
> As King of blis;
> I am so semely, blode and bone,
> My sete shall be there as was his.

> Say, felows, how semys now me
> To sit in seyte of Trynyte?
> I am so bright of ich a lym,
> I trow me seme as well as hym.

But to make Lucifer the main figure, as the centralizing of his fall would dictate, could not possibly square with Milton's final choice of the human theme of Everyman. Once Lucifer's fall is ruled out, only Eve's can be considered the logical centre of the plot: for Adam's fall was conditioned by Eve's and is hence subordinate; and without Eve's fall there would have been no anticipatory offer by the Son to be a ransom,

---

[1] On the other hand C. G. Osgood in *Poetry as a Means of Grace* (Princeton, 1941), 100, sees that the drama extends uninterrupted till Adam and Eve repent in Book Ten.

no effusion of heavenly Grace after, and no world history. In her fall Heaven and Hell meet in conflict. So, as far as the plot goes, Raleigh ought to be right.

But abstracted plot and actual poetry are different things, and we should not assume that they must each evolve with the same emphasis. And if we read *Paradise Lost* rightly, opening ourselves to the poetry, we shall find that Eve's eating the apple is by no means the one, exclusive, centre of the poem. There are reasons why in actual practice a poet would find it hard to make it so.

In the bare story Eve was sinless till the precise moment when she reached out her rash hand and plucked the fruit.[1] Milton may have intended to substantiate the story. He does indeed say that she was still sinless when she had so far yielded to the serpent's blandishments as to follow him to the tree whose fruit he had been advertising so skilfully. But intentions could be of no avail against the terms to which Milton submitted himself by offering to present in ample narrative the transition from a state of innocence to a state of sin. Under the terms of the story these two realms must be separated by a definite but dimensionless frontier: there cannot be a no-man's-land between; in the passage, time must not count. Such a lightning-quick change might be effective in a film; as mentioned above, it showed itself to be possible in the simple form of the Miracle Plays; but in a narrative poem it could only be ridiculous, and in his heart Milton knew that well enough.

In Book Four of *Paradise Lost* Milton pictured his state of innocence, and it is one of the most lovely and thrilling pictures in all poetry. But he could not possibly have conducted his account of the Fall with that picture for sole starting-point; the effect would have been sudden and violent and would have carried no conviction. And he makes no such attempt. Instead he resorts to some faking: perfectly legitimate in a poem, yet faking nevertheless. He anticipates the

---

[1] With the argument that follows compare Waldock, *Paradise Lost and its Critics* (Cambridge, 1947), 61: 'Adam and Eve must already be fallen (technically) before they can begin to fall.'

10

Fall by attributing to Eve and Adam feelings which though nominally felt in the state of innocence are actually not compatible with it.[1] The first stage is Eve's dream at the beginning of Book Five, an episode which, it is recognized, duplicates in its small way the greater temptation in Book Nine. Here Satan insinuates the insidious (and characteristically Cavalier) sentiment of 'suffer thyself to be admired', urging her to walk out in the night so that all heaven's eyes may admire her beauty. She is then made to imagine herself seeking Adam and finding herself suddenly by the 'Tree of interdicted Knowledge'. She sees to her horror an angelic shape eat the fruit, boast of its virtue, and make her eat too, on the plea that she will become a goddess. Having eaten, she seems to fly up to heaven and see the earth beneath her. In her wonder at her flight her dream ends. Adam does his best to comfort Eve, giving her a reassuringly academic account of the way dreams happen and ending with the general principle that *should* clear Eve of all offense:

> Evil into the mind of God or Man
> May come and go, so unapprov'd, and leave
> No spot or blame behind.

This means[2] that into the mind of angel or man evil may enter, and, if it is repudiated, fail to incriminate. In the abstract the doctrine may be tenable, but it cannot work in concrete literary presentation. No human being can conceive or represent evil entering a mind quite alien to it. Dramatically, the mere fact of entrance implies some pre-existing sympathy. And, in actual dramatic truth, Eve, though not approving the implication of her dream, does by her symptoms imply that it has touched her, that it is far from alien; for Adam, waking out of the light sleep of perfect innocence, is surprised

---

[1] Milton does the same with Mammon in i, 680–4. Even in Heaven, while yet unfallen, Mammon was more interested in the gold of Heaven's pavement than in the beatific vision. Such an interest in the heart of one of the principal angels shows him already fallen. But who minds in the reading or blames Milton for faking to the advantage of the poetry?

[2] See Maurice Kelley, *This Great Argument* (Princeton, 1941), 77.

> to find unwak'nd *Eve*
> With Tresses discompos'd, and glowing cheek,
> As through unquiet rest.

And if the dream has disturbed Eve so much, she has really passed from a state of innocence to one of sin. This is not to blame Milton. He is confronted with an impossibility; and to achieve dramatic poetry at all he has to fake. And he has succeeded as well as a man, in the circumstances, can. We do accept, as we read, Milton's specious plea that Adam and Eve satisfy the conditions of nominal innocence required by the story; and with another part of our mind we know that Eve is really, even if only a little way, on the far side of the line that divides innocence from experience.

Eve having made the transition, it was necessary for Adam to do the same. And he does it at the end of Book Eight when he confides to Raphael how Eve's beauty is apt to affect his mind in a way that is dangerous to the sovereignty there of the Reason. Not that Adam denies this sovereignty, but by speaking of his transport of love for Eve as 'commotion strange', he has admitted to feelings alien to the angelic and akin to Eve's sleeping perturbation. Technically, he is still innocent, but in our hearts we recognize him as just across the frontier. Nor is he straightforward in his dealings with Raphael. When rebuked by Raphael for allowing Eve's physical charms to create in him the illusion of her wisdom, he neither answers nor admits the rebuke but merely shifts his ground and says that it is rather her delightful manners that have this effect. He then, with something near impudence, counterattacks and asks if the angels love too.[1] Adam shows great charm and mental dexterity. The irony was that Eve was to treat him, her superior, exactly as Adam here treats

[1] See the excellent analysis of these speeches by Paul Turner in *English Studies*, 1948, 1–5, where he disagrees with Waldock's contention that it is Raphael who misunderstands Adam (A. J. A. Waldock, *op. cit.* 43–4). But Turner underrates Adam's loverlike fervour as Waldock overrates it. Surely the poetic virtue lies in the ambivalence: Raphael's rebuke was just, Adam's love (in a man virtually fallen) was also good up to a point. Just so the loves of Paolo and Francesca were noble up to a point. Yet they merited their infernal punishment.

his superior, Raphael, when they argue about separate or joint garden-work in the next book. My main point is that both are virtually fallen before the official temptation has begun.

A further advance into the realm of experience is effected by means of the smoke-screen generated by the great prologue to Book Nine. Having there announced that he is changing his notes to tragic, Milton can risk presenting us with an Adam and Eve more human still than the two episodes just mentioned could dictate. Although ignorant as yet of the more violent human passions, Adam and Eve conduct their dispute about separate or joint gardening as evolved human beings such as we know.

The Fall, then, must be extended back in time; it has no plain and sensational beginning; and the actual eating of the apple becomes no more than an emphatic stage in a process already begun, the stage when the darker and stormier passions make their entry into the human heart.

The same is true of what happens after Eve has eaten the apple. The process of falling continues. It takes time for it to work itself utterly out. Indeed it could be maintained that the Fall is not accomplished, does not in deepest verity take place, till Adam's great despairing speech late in Book Ten (line 720), ending:

> O Conscience, into what Abyss of fears
> And horrors hast thou driv'n me; out of which
> I find no way, from deep to deeper plung'd.

By that time indeed Adam's education in the knowledge of good and evil is complete.

Raleigh's point of radiation, then, turns out in the poem itself not to be a point at all but an inseparable item in a substantial area of the whole poem. But once this is granted, it will be found that another theme has been added to, or intertwined with, the theme of the Fall; intertwined so firmly as to be inextricable: the theme of regeneration. Long before the effects of the Fall have made themselves fully felt, the process of regeneration has begun. It begins, although the characters in whom it operates are not conscious of it, when, early in Book Ten, the Son, having pronounced his judgment on the actors in the Fall, pities Adam and Eve and clothes their nakedness. And it reaches obvious fruition when, at the end of the book, Adam and Eve make peace with each other and confess their errors to God.

It comes then to this. Instead of a small spot in Book Nine for a watershed you have to take the whole great area of Books Nine and Ten. That Milton intended these to go together is evident from the way he concludes them: one end is the pendant of the other. Book Nine ends with the unresolved quarrelling of Adam and Eve:

> Thus they in mutual accusation spent
> The fruitless hours, but neither self-condemning,
> And of their vain contest appear'd no end.

Book Ten comes to rest with the contrasted picture of Adam and Eve reconciled in mutual amity and common humility, seeking the pardon of God:

> So spake our Father penitent, nor *Eve*
> Felt less remorse: they forthwith to the place
> Repairing where he judg'd them prostrate fell
> Before him reverent, and both confess'd
> Humbly their faults, and pardon begg'd, with tears
> Watering the ground, and with their sighs the Air
> Frequenting, sent from hearts contrite, in sign
> Of sorrow unfeign'd, and humiliation meek.

The habit, then, of subordinating Book Ten to Book Nine, is mistaken; and if you argue from such an assumption you may do violence to what the poetry should be telling you. And that is the fundamental question: to what does the poetry point? But only a fairly detailed account of the text can answer it. I turn therefore to an account of Books Nine and Ten of *Paradise Lost*, as I have come to read them.

In this account I shall attribute to Milton's treatment of Adam's and Eve's psychology a subtlety not usually allowed. At the same time I acknowledge the force of T. S. Eliot's recent pronouncement on them:

They are the original *Man* and *Woman*, not types, but proto-types: if they were not set apart from ordinary humanity they would not be Adam and Eve. They have the general charac-teristics of men and women, such that we can recognize, in the temptation and the fall, the first motions of the faults and virtues, the abjection and nobility, of all their descendants. They have ordinary humanity to the right degree, and yet are not, and should not be, ordinary mortals. Were they more particularized they would be false, and if Milton had been more interested in humanity, he could not have created them.[1]

That is finely said, and it is mainly true. But at least Milton must be allowed to have been greatly interested in the human relation of man and wife. The triumph is that he can be so subtle and perceptive and yet not destroy the pair's essential generality. I turn to Milton's text.

The eighth book of *Paradise Lost* closes the long central episode of Raphael's visit to Paradise. It also shows night falling on the last happy day there; as he says:

> But I can now no more; the parting Sun
> Beyond the Earths green Cape and verdant Isles
> Hesperean sets, my signal to depart.

And his last words to Adam—

> And all temptation to transgress repel—

are a solemn warning that looks forward to the next book.

The great prologue to the ninth book both carries our minds back to the opening of the poem with its theme of dis-obedience and announces the entrance of the tragic. Milton has now to introduce his actors and he rightly begins with Satan. It was in Hell that the action began in Book One; it is right that Satan should begin it in the culminating books. And it is, for the time being, not the quite degraded Satan, the Satan who took the form of a toad to spit evil dreams into Eve's ear, but the bad creature still haunted by his remembrance of the good. His great soliloquy betrays an exquisite aesthetic sense,

[1] *Milton*, British Academy Lecture for 1947, pp. 10–11.

which now serves only to torture him. He is overcome by the beauty of the earth (line 103).

> Terrestrial Heav'n, danc't round by other Heav'ns
> That shine, yet bear their bright officious Lamps,
> Light above Light, for thee alone, as seems,
> In thee concentring all their precious beams
> Of sacred influence . . .
> With what delight could I have walkt thee round,
> If I could joy in aught, sweet interchange
> Of Hill, and Vallie, Rivers, Woods and Plaines;
> . . . . . . but I in none of these
> Find place or refuge.

And Satan has still refinement enough to hate the degradation of having to take the shape of a beast:

> O foul descent! that I who erst contended
> With Gods to sit the highest, am now constraind
> Into a Beast, and mixt with bestial slime,
> This essence to incarnate and imbrute.

And the very capaciousness of his mind makes him the more formidable adversary. He arrives at Eden in the night, finds out the serpent, whom he has already chosen among all animals as the fittest for his purpose, takes possession of him, asleep, and awaits the dawn.

The dawn breaks; all creatures, plant beast and man, send up their praise to God; and the fateful conversation between Adam and Eve about the strategy of their morning's gardening begins. Look at their total conversation (lines 204–384), and several things emerge. From first to last Eve takes and keeps the initiative, though she very nearly loses it at the end. Her speeches are short, clear, and emphatic, and her mind is working very fast. Adam, on the other hand, is unprepared, laborious, and on the defensive, although he warms up and becomes really cogent at the end. It is a state of affairs both entirely realistic and clean contrary to the ideal picture in Book Four where Adam's 'fair large front and eye sublime declared absolute rule' and Eve's curls declared submission. The natural hierarchy has already been upset. The speeches themselves are highly dramatic, and they come from two fully equipped human beings like ourselves.

Eve begins with her proposal that since they waste so much time taking notice of each other they should garden separately and thus get more done in the time. It comes out pat and has the air of having been thought out beforehand. The proposal was relatively harmless but it was not sincere. The pair were still in the honeymoon stage, and the last thing Eve really wanted was to be separated even for a morning from her lover. So she lays a mild trap for Adam, hoping that he will not fall into it but will retort that she asks too much and that he cannot bear to lose sight of her. That she was not sincere is evident from the deliberately contrasted proposal Milton puts into her mouth after the Fall and when they have repented:

> But the Field
> To labour calls us now with sweat impos'd,
> Though after sleepless Night; for see the Morn,
> All unconcern'd with our unrest, begins
> Her rosie progress smiling; let us forth,
> I never from thy side henceforth to stray,
> Wherere our days work lies. (xi, 171–7.)

Here Eve not only proposes to work with Adam, but is really anxious that they should do as much as possible. The exact reverse would be the case before.

Adam, after the manner of men when sleepy or not at their best, falls into the trap, taking Eve at her word, and proceeds to make two mistakes. Instead of being personal, he is vague and lectures her on the abstract principle of recreation, rather as if he were a seventeenth-century undergraduate upholding the thesis that work prospers best when interspersed with play. And then, not noticing her disappointment and her consequent deafness to argument, he chooses the wrong moment to advance his really important plea of danger and the folly of being separated when they know a foe may be at hand. And he ends earnestly but on the wrong note:

> Leave not the faithful side
> That gave thee being, still shades thee and protects,

> The Wife, where danger or dishonour lurks,
> Safest and seemliest by her Husband stands,
> Who guards her, or with her the worst endures.

Such apparent self-praise from Adam could hardly be soothing just then. Eve stands on her dignity and, her mind working very clearly and freely, makes a brilliant and telling retort. She replies with 'sweet austeer composure' that Adam plainly does not trust her and that this is an unfair slight on her character:

> But that thou shouldst my firmness therefore doubt
> To God or thee, because we have a foe
> May tempt it, I expected not to hear.

Of course Adam had not quite meant that, but how difficult to deal clearly and briefly with so dangerous a simplification! However, he sees he must do something to propitiate Eve and replies with 'healing words'. Even so, he begins badly, with the poor plea that he does not really fear that Eve will fall but that he fears the slur on her honour which any attempt on her firmness must imply; a very weak shift of ground and a shoddy piece of improvisation. However, it has given him time to collect his wits and he at last says something really effective: that he needs her help every bit as much as she needs his:

> I from the influence of thy looks receave
> Access in every Vertue, in thy sight
> More wise, more watchful, stronger, if need were
> Of outward strength.

There is still hope that Adam may save the situation, and Milton lets us know that Adam is now really doing his best, when he adds

> So spake domestick *Adam* in his care
> And Matrimonial Love.

Eve naturally is not to be appeased at once, and she goes on to score more points. She cannot agree that the mere attempt will scathe her honour; it is the foiled tempter who will be

18

dishonoured. Heaven, the only criterion that matters, will approve. And she turns on Adam those doctrines of freedom reminiscent of *Areopagitica*, which she had doubtless learnt from his own lips:

> And what is Faith, Love, Vertue unassaid
> Alone, without exterior help sustaind?

Her speech is brief, decisive, masterly. But it is nevertheless wrong, for she confounds the sin of asking for trouble with the virtue of not avoiding the dust and heat when these are necessary. Adam is by now thoroughly roused, and his real intellectual superiority asserts itself. He grasps Eve's mistake, but forbears scoring off her. Instead he replies with fervour and humility. God supplied us, he argues, with the necessary armour against evil. But it should be used discreetly. You cannot be too careful: for the will may go wrong through the reason's acting on false data, through thinking false appearances to be the truth. And he really answers Eve when he says:

> Seek not temptation then, which to avoide
> Were better, and most likelie if from me
> Thou sever not: Trial will come unsought.

And he preaches the true contemporary and Miltonic doctrine when he says:

> Wouldst thou approve thy constancie, approve
> First thy obedience.

In other words, respect the natural leadership of the husband. Adam has been eloquent; we know that Eve must have been impressed. Indeed when she makes her next (and last) speech, she is 'submiss'. Adam really has the situation in hand. Eve has got not what she first wanted but something to take its place. She first wanted a small tribute to her charm; now she has had the satisfaction of rousing Adam and of obtaining a degree of attention she had never expected. And then comes the tragedy. Adam, who could now be firm with impunity, whom Eve expects to be firm, suddenly weakens.

He goes on to find a specious argument why in this instance separation may be better, misapplies the doctrine of liberty, and almost recommends Eve to go against his true wishes. His argument is: it may now be that, having been warned so thoroughly, you will in isolation be better able to resist temptation than in the security and lack of vigilance that would follow on our being together. It is a false argument, because both of them are now thoroughly warned and there is no reason why the effect of the warning should wear off in each other's company.

Adam's misguided lenience makes things hard for Eve. She would now like to yield, but after all her protests it is hardly consonant with proper pride for her not to accept his offer. So she accepts it, and as a compromise says she does so in deference to Adam's final hypothesis. The whole situation is pervaded with tragic irony. Adam weakens just when he could so easily have been strong. Eve, having requested to garden alone, gains her request just as she has repented of it. With this important phase of the Fall Satan has had nothing to do: it has been conducted on the Meredithian principle:

> In tragic life, God wot,
> No villain need be! Passions spin the plot:
> We are betrayed by what is false within.

What, it may be asked, was Adam's motive in giving way? Perhaps mistaken chivalry. When he saw Eve yielding, he could not bear not to meet her half way. And the chivalry was stimulated by her surpassing charm. Like Bunyan's Christiana, Eve was a woman of quick apprehension. While baffling Adam's superior intelligence by her quickness she must have been highly attractive; and she has her temper in perfect control throughout. But her charm and the air of comedy that it creates do not prevent the essential tragedy or the hard fact that both Adam and Eve have sinned: Eve by assuming the leadership that Milton's age believed belonged in nature to the male, Adam in failing in the authority it was his duty to assert.

There follows one of the great moments of the poem, the

description of Eve walking away from Adam with her gardening tools. It is in Milton's most delicate and enchanting vein and it gains in poignancy by being set between the tragic irony just described and the author's lament for Eve that her peace of mind is gone for ever:

> O much deceav'd, much failing, hapless *Eve*,
> Of thy presum'd return! event perverse!
> Thou never from that houre in Paradise
> Foundst either sweet repast, or sound repose.

Whether Milton meant it consciously or not, we should surely in reading these words think of what Iago said as he saw Othello approach, to be caught inevitably in his trap:

> Not Poppy, nor Mandragora,
> Nor all the drowsie Syrrups of the world,
> Shall ever medicine thee to that sweete sleep
> Which thou owd'st yesterday.

With the temptation itself, culminating in Adam and Eve eating the fruit, I shall deal more briefly. It has been handled over and over again, and the very attraction it holds out for unceasing reinterpretation proves how rich it is in content, how successful Milton was in making it interesting and inexhaustible. It would be going too far to say that all the interpretations are right, but it is true that more interpretations are simultaneously right than the single propounders of their own interpretations are prepared to admit, at least while in the act of writing up their pet notion. To such a failing I must plead guilty when putting the Fall mainly in terms of mental triviality in my *Milton*.[1] Not that I now think this motive to be absent. Milton does insist that Eve failed to grasp the issue through a kind of levity, and such an insistence accords perfectly with a train of thought running through many of his pamphlets: that what defeats human betterment is a kind of blindness to the issues. Nor is the sin of triviality a trivial sin. To quote from one of the most eminent modern novelists, the late L. H. Myers:

[1] I admit the foree of Maurice Kelley's rebuke (*This Great Argument*, 150, note 31).

If triviality takes an important place in the world, if it is the chief barrier between men and God, then triviality is important. . . . No corruption is more easily spread than that of trivial-mindedness. It is more wicked to be heedless of good and evil than to say: Evil be thou my good! The man who defies God thereby acknowledges Him, and for him salvation waits; but the man who ignores God, the man who is incapable of an emotional response to the universe in its august or divine aspect—that man is indeed beyond the pale.

Nevertheless, I may have appeared to narrow the motives overmuch to this single one. Certainly I should now admit a number of other motives. A good deal has been said about the faculties of the understanding and the will in Milton's version of the Fall; and there is no doubt that, following St Paul and St Augustine, Milton showed Eve sinning through a defect of the understanding and Adam of the will. Indeed Milton probably turned the difficulty inherent in his myth of having two tragic heroes into the profit of being able to express through this duality the traditional division of the human mind into wit and will. Anyhow Milton tells us that Adam did understand the issue (at least up to a point), that he was not deceived but was overcome by female charm. That Milton meant Eve to go wrong through a defective understanding is plain from the words Adam addresses to her in his last speech before they part (ix, 351):

> But God left free the Will, for what obeys
> Reason, is free, and Reason he made right
> But bid her well beware, and still erect,
> Least by some faire appearing good surpris'd
> She dictate false, and misinforme the Will
> To do what God expressly hath forbid.

These words do in the main foreshadow the process of Eve's temptation. Her reason is deceived by the Serpent's pretence that as he, a dumb beast, has by eating the fruit risen to the human faculty of speech, so she, if she eats, will attain a correspondingly superior state. And her will answers to the false premises submitted to it by the understanding. The species of temptation Eve undergoes comes out plainly if you contrast her with Spenser's Sir Guyon in Mammon's Cave. There, it was a pure question of will, of the will resisting the passions. Sir Guyon knew that it was the principle that mattered, that if he touched the tiniest piece of gold the fiend would get him as surely as if he trundled away a barrow-load.

But in speaking of wit and will we must beware of simplifying, for Eve's will was swayed by her passions as well as by the misguidance of her intellect, and Adam allowed his intellect to sleep as well as submitting his will to his passion for Eve; for Eve's desire to be promoted in the natural scale was a passion, and Adam before eating the fruit, which he had already decided to do for love of Eve, half-fools his understanding with a piece of wishful thinking:

> Perhaps the Fact
> Is not so hainous now, foretasted Fruit
> Profan'd first by the Serpent, by him first
> Made common and unhallowed ere our taste;
> Nor yet on him found deadly, he yet lives,
> Lives, as thou saidst, and gaines to live as Man
> Higher degree of Life, inducement strong
> To us, as likely tasting to attaine
> Proportional ascent.

As we must avoid a narrow interpretation of motives, so must we of the crime itself. Milton himself, in the formidable list he gives in the *De Doctrina* of the crimes the eating of the apple implied, should keep us right here. But it is not simply a question of what crimes the prime sin of disobedience brought with it but one of how the sin itself is to be interpreted. I have to confess to making too little of the disobedience in my *Milton*, because I took it in the Addisonian sense and found that sense too impoverished to fit Milton's conceptions. That part of the crime involved in Milton's version of the Fall was simple disobedience to the ascertainable mandate of God is undoubted. But that does not mean that Milton considered the mandates of God so easily ascertainable as Addison and his age thought them. Nor does simple disobedience of a simple arbitrary command anywhere near cover the total meaning of disobedience to Milton. Its wider and more pervasive meaning is a breaking of the natural order as prescribed by God. Just as Satan had aspired, through pride, beyond his natural archangelic state to sheer godhead, so he tempted Eve to eat the forbidden fruit that she might transcend her natural human limitations. Adam also offends against the natural order by failing to maintain the hierarchical principle in his dealings with Eve. Whether or not Milton compels us to sympathize with Adam when he refuses to forsake Eve in her extremity, at least we can join with him in deploring Adam's crucial weakness, as described above, in allowing Eve to go away unprotected. And in the end Adam joins Eve in imagining that the forbidden fruit is bringing them nearer to godhead. Such disobedience is near to what is now popularly described as the acts of disregarding the facts of existence, going against the nature of things, or refusing to come to terms with the conditions of one's environment. And it is just because a large part of the Fall's meaning stands for something so simple and fundamental as this that the heart of *Paradise Lost* can never be superannuated.

Of course to Milton the 'nature of things' was other than to us: he inherited a belief in the grand, defined, diversified, and fantastic array of supposed facts that went to make up the Elizabethan world picture. But no change in the world picture can stale the notion that a large portion of wisdom is to understand the conditions of life and to submit ourselves freely to them. Thence comes true liberty. There is the initial liberty to revolt or not to revolt: common to all men. But revolt or disobedience is the loss of liberty, while acceptance of things as they are is the true fulfilment of it. Within that acceptance the greatest measure of legitimate choice will be attained.

But I have spent time enough on Milton's supposed notions as abstracted from his text; and I return to my main business, the text itself.

By rising so high in his description of Eve parting from Adam, Milton set himself an exalted standard, but he excels himself. He describes the garden with a beauty equal to that of the original description in Book Four, yet with greater intimacy as from within. Eve, working among the roses, is perfectly set in the natural beauty:

> Veild in a Cloud of Fragrance, where she stood,
> Half spi'd, so thick the Roses bushing round
> About her glowd.

And Satan's momentary relaxation, when he surveys the scene,

> Stupidly good, of enemitie disarm'd,

and his returning hate serve brilliantly to space Eve's fateful conversation with Adam from her culminating conversation with Satan.

This second conversation has been sufficiently described and admired. Its drift is clear. Satan relies on sheer flattery and on airing the temptation to aspire beyond one's lot. His grand argument is that *he* has done so and succeeded—

> And life more perfect have attaind than Fate
> Meant me, by ventring higher than my Lot.

It may not have been seen how much irony the conversation contains, mainly through its contrasts with Eve's other conversation that morning. The legitimate praise of which Adam unluckily had starved her is made good by the gross flattery of the Devil. If Eve temporarily upset Adam by the quickness of her thought, the Devil pays her back treble in her own coin in his final harangue. Waldock has shown excellently with what blinding effect Satan shifts from one premise to another to draw his specious conclusions. And finally there is an irony in the Devil's Pauline phraseology when he recommends the new life that the fruit will promote:

> So ye shall die perhaps, by putting off
> Human, to put on Gods, death to be wisht.

Satan as it were parodies by anticipation Paul's exhortations to die to sin, to put off the old man and put on the new.

The impetus that carries the action to Eve's eating the fruit is both worthy of the scenes that precede it and makes no pause at that point. On the contrary it presses right on, Milton spending no more than two and a half lines in describing Nature's lament at the Fall. There is no warrant in the actual poem for centring everything just here: on the contrary Eve's progress in sin is continued and intensified after she eats the fruit. She now proceeds to the sin of idolatry by praising the forbidden fruit as divine and then doing obeisance to it; and she identifies herself with Satan by repeating his most outrageous assertion: that the tree was not God's creation at all and hence not in the Gods' power to give or forbid,

> For had the gift bin theirs, it had not here
> Thus grown.

But as her speech proceeds and she thinks of Adam, the tone modulates and acquires a touch of that domestic comedy which had not been absent from her talk with Adam that same morning:

> But to *Adam* in what sort
> Shall I appear? shall I to him make known
> As yet my change, and give him to partake
> Full happiness with me, or rather not,
> But keep the odds of knowledge in my power
> Without Copartner? so to add what wants
> In Female Sex, the more to draw his Love,
> And render me more equal, and perhaps,
> A thing not undesirable, sometime
> Superior; for inferior who is free?
> This may be well: but what if God have seen,
> And Death ensue? then I shall be no more,
> And *Adam* wedded to another *Eve*,
> Shall live with her enjoying, I extinct;
> A death to think. Confirm'd then I resolve,
> *Adam* shall share with me in bliss or woe.

If you heed the sense alone and not the tone and feeling of these lines, you can turn them into a sheer exhibition of evil motives. C. S. Lewis has gone so far as to make them include the sin of murder. Of course they show Eve outrageously seeking to upset the natural order. But surely the lightened

rhythm and the ironically delicate human observation forbid
us to press them to the utmost solemnity. Eve's speech contains just the same doctrine as this stanza from Chaucer's
Troilus and Criseyde.

> As proude Bayard ginneth for to skippe
> Out of the wey, so priketh him his corn,
> Till he a lash have of the longe whippe,
> Than thenketh he, 'though I praunce al biforn
> First in the trays, ful fat and newe shorn,
> Yet I am but an hors, and horses lawe
> I moot endure, and with my feres drawe.'

As the whip persuades Bayard, full of oats, not to aspire beyond horsehood, so inversely the fruit has intoxicated Eve to
aspire beyond womanhood, and we know she will rue it. But
it would take more than C. S. Lewis to reduce Chaucer's passage to gravity. And, whether we like it or not, *some* comedy
has crept into Milton's treatment of the Fall. Why should this
be? Perhaps he wishes, even thus early, to reassure us that all
is not irretrievably lost, and that Eve's wicked thoughts must
be viewed in proportion, that they do not really exclude all
chance of better ones. After all Milton was not one of those
Calvinists who believed that the Fall extinguished every
spark of virtue in the human heart. But I fancy there is also a
structural reason. Milton has by now been at a high pitch of
intensity for a long time, and to continue so just here would
be to make the eating of the fruit indeed the exclusive climax
of the poem. It is just because he does not intend this that the
pitch is now relaxed.

Nor does the intensity really grow in the scene when Adam
also eats. Eve's speech to him is splendidly dramatic. We see
her flushed face and hear her unnaturally fluent plausibility
hiding the embarrassment and fear. There is little elaboration
in Adam's yielding to her wishes and his resolve to stand by
her. His horror, though nobly, is very briefly described and
in a conventional, neo-classic[1] manner:

[1] For the neo-classic character of the passage and its relation to Statius see
Appendix A, *Milton and Statius* (p. 170).

> Adam, soon as he heard
> The fatal Trespass don by Eve, amaz'd.
> Astonied stood and Blank, while horror chill
> Ran through his veins, and all his joynts relax'd;
> From his slack hand the Garland wreath'd for Eve
> Down drop'd, and all the faded Roses shed.

Had Milton wanted emphasis and elaboration here, how easily could he have made Adam pause over his choice, wavering agonizingly this way and that. Instead, Adam seems to have made his choice beforehand, to have decided from the first that if Eve fell he would not forsake her. Certainly his decision is definite and unhesitating and has been taken without the least pressure from Eve:

> some cursed fraud
> Of Enemie hath beguiled thee, yet unknown,
> And me with thee hath ruind, for with thee
> Certain my resolution is to Die;
> How can I live without thee, how forgoe
> Thy sweet Converse and Love so dearly joyn'd,
> To live again in these wilde woods forlorn?
> Should God create another *Eve*, and I
> Another Rib afford, yet loss of thee
> Would never from my heart; no, no, I feel
> The Link of Nature chain me: Flesh of Flesh,
> Bone of my Bone thou art, and from thy State
> Mine never shall be parted, bliss or woe. (ix, 904.)

No lines in Milton have been more discussed than these; and I should like particularly to mention Waldock's[1] remarks on them. I agree with him that as poetry and in their context these lines compel us to sympathize with Adam's love for Eve as manifested in them. It is equally clear that by the nominal requirements of the scheme we should be shocked and horrified; for what more shocking than the spectacle of a man, still innocent, choosing to flout God with his eyes open and to sacrifice eternal principles for an impulse to companionship? Yet in actual reading we are not profoundly shocked, and the reason is that Adam's innocence at this point is only nominal.

[1] *Paradise Lost and its Critics* (Cambridge, 1947), 46.

As pointed out above, he has really crossed the frontier, and no abstention from eating the fruit can put him back the other side. The nature of Adam's action can best be seen by the analogy of a man who hates war and yet consents to fight. To fight is bad, yet not to fight is worse because it is a denial of the common human fate, of an incrimination it is as yet impossible for any human being to be free of. To keep clear on narrowly personal moral grounds would be to incur a self-righteousness worse than the taint of association in an evil which all humanity is doomed to share. That, I maintain, is a true analogy as dictated by the poetical effect. That it can easily be disproved by the doctrine of the poem in isolation from the poetry is a minor affair. Once again we have to do with a discrepancy with which Milton was powerless to deal except by faking. And if we follow the lead of the poetry, we can only admire him for doing as well as he does.

Having uttered to himself his memorable resolution to die with Eve, Adam turns his words to her 'in calm mood' and proceeds to put best face on her action that he can. Thus Milton continues the less intense strain that began with the intrusion of comedy, but at a price: there is something just a little starved about the account of Adam's fall. Animation rises when Eve blesses Adam for his resolution and weeps for gratitude and joy. And yet Milton does not allow the human feeling to go uncriticized. As he had previously tempered Eve's exhibition of criminal thoughts with comedy, so contrariwise he now corrects her effusion of understandable but all too fallibly human feelings with a stern reminder of the pair's fundamental incrimination.

> So saying, she embrac'd him, and for joy
> Tenderly wept, much won that he his Love
> Had so enobl'd, as of choice to incurr
> Divine displeasure for her sake, or Death.[1]

[1] It is a few lines later that Milton describes Adam as not deceived but fondly overcome by female charm (lines 998–9). In my *Milton* I called the sentiment inconsistent with what went before because Adam had made up his mind before Eve exercised her charms on him (p. 263). I now agree with Paul Turner (*l.c.* 14) that 'female charm' refers not to Eve's caresses at this point but to the previous influence of her physical attractions. Adam, in fact, has put into action the state of mind Raphael reproved at the end of Book Eight.

Nothing could be finer than the implied ironic comparison between his act as it appeared to her and as it appears *sub specie aeternitatis*. Nor does Milton's stern comment invalidate the sympathy he has made the reader feel with Adam's choice to stand by Eve; for that comment can apply by now to the whole process of the Fall as it began in Eve's dream and to fallen humanity in general and its pitiful deficiencies.

The ensuing description of how the fruit intoxicated the pair is admirable. Comedy re-enters but more grimly, in Adam's profane wish that God might have forbidden ten trees instead of one and in the description of their falling into lust. Then they sleep, and when they wake find their innocence lost and know themselves to be naked.

In describing how Adam and Eve waked to shame Milton was faced with difficulties. He had to recount their shame of nakedness, for it is so prominent in *Genesis*, being in fact the principal effect of eating the fruit. He meets his difficulty by making their shame go far beyond nakedness, and he reinforces the theme of the nakedness by introducing their act of lust. Even so, Milton's account is not very explicit; but it can be legitimately made so, if we set it in the total context of the poem. Adam and Eve had dropped off to sleep in the deceptive confidence that they were growing into gods; they woke into the rueful realization that they were less than their normal selves, suffering from a hangover. They had not experienced deceit previously (even if they were in some sense fallen, before they actually tasted the fruit) and that was part of their innocence: now they know the shame of having been tricked. Other motives of shame have to do with their appetites. Instead of eating their noontide dinner in a decent orderly way they had indulged in a premature, extemporary, and intoxicating picnic. Instead of waiting till evening and the ceremonious sequestration of their nuptial bower, where no animal dared come, they had indulged in a hasty, unceremonious fit of love: exactly what Milton in his great panegyric on married love had called 'casual fruition' and had associated with harlots. When we think of these contrasts we may understand how the sexual act has been soiled for them and how they become conscious of their nakedness. It is to be noted that Adam and Eve have forgotten God. Shame for disobedience does not enter in. They are self-centred.

The book ends with the loosening of the full range of personal human passions and the pair's mutual recrimination. It is a quite masterly ending, terribly true to ordinary human nature, and too sad to be called comic. It brings no pause in the action; the effects of the Fall are only beginning to make themselves felt.

Book Ten marks, not a new action, but the transfer of the existing action from the bounds of Paradise to the whole universe. The full incidence of the Fall remains to be described. That incidence is double: on the whole world outside, and back again on Adam and Eve through the evocation of heavenly grace. This book is thus both cosmic and domestic, and for range and variety it excels all others in the poem. Whether it is the finest of all the books need not be debated; at least it is the worthy setting for what I now believe the culmination of the poem.

First the Fall is reported in heaven, and the Son descends to the garden to pronounce judgment. Adam and Eve are tied up in their own shame and barren passions:

> Love was not in their looks, either to God
> Or to each other, but apparent guilt,
> And shame, and perturbation, and despaire,
> Anger, and obstinacie, and hate, and guile.

And the Son's merciful bearing in pronouncing judgment, and his active charity in giving them clothes, make no impression on their conscious minds. To all appearances Hell has triumphed completely in them; after which it is but fitting that the further triumphs of Hell should be recounted.

There follows (line 229) one of the grandest of all episodes in the poem: the building by Sin and Death of the causeway from Hell to the universe. Since its richness of connotation may not have been fully recognized, I will comment on it at some length. Milton describes how Sin and Death, waiting at Hell's gate, sense the change that has been brought about by the Fall and know that they may now range the earth freely. To connect Hell and earth better they build a causeway from hell-gate over chaos to the zenith of the universe, where there is the entrance from space into the outermost bounding sphere of the whole cosmic system. This is also the point whence the way to heaven ascends. They construct the bridge through the deathlike operation of the qualities of cold and dry.

As well as grand the episode is grotesque. And it is so, partly because it is a parody: a parody of God's creating the world in Book Seven. Here are the lines describing the work on the causeway, Death having spoken:

> So saying, with delight he snuff'd the smell
> Of mortal change on Earth. As when a flock
> Of ravenous Fowl, though many a League remote,
> Against the day of Battel, to a Field,
> Where armies lie encampt, come flying, lur'd
> With sent of living Carcasses design'd
> For death, the following day, in bloodie fight.
> So sented the grim Feature, and upturn'd
> His Nostril wide into the murkie Air,
> Sagacious of his Quarry from so farr.
> Then Both from out Hell Gates into the waste
> Wide Anarchie of *Chaos* damp and dark
> Flew divers, and with Power (their Power was great)
> Hovering upon the Waters: what they met
> Solid or slimie, as in raging Sea
> Tost up and down, together crowded drove
> From each side shoaling towards the mouth of Hell.
> As when two Polar Winds blowing adverse
> Upon the Cronian Sea, together drive
> Mountains of Ice, that stop th'imagin'd way
> Beyond Petsora Eastward, to the rich
> Cathaian Coast. The aggregated Soyle
> Death with his Mace petrific, cold and dry,
> As with a Trident smote, and fix't as firm
> As Delos floating once; the rest his look
> Bound with Gorgonian rigor not to move,
> And with Asphaltic slime; broad as the Gate,
> Deep to the Roots of Hell the gathr'd beach
> They fasten'd, and the Mole immense wrought on

> Over the foaming deep high Archt a Bridge
> Of length prodigious joyning to the Wall
> Immoveable of this now fenceless world
> Forfeit to Death; from hence a passage broad,
> Smooth, easie, inoffensive down to Hell.[1]

Though Sin and Death are not actually called vultures, yet, when you add the initial simile to the later adjective *hovering*, it is clear you are meant thus to picture them. Compare now the corresponding description lines 210–242, in Book Seven, of the Son and the Spirit going out from heaven to create.

> On heavn'ly ground they stood, and from the shore
> They view'd the vast immeasurable Abyss
> Outrageous as a Sea, dark, wasteful, wilde,
> Up from the bottom turn'd by furious windes
> And surging waves, as Mountains to assault
> Heav'ns highth, and with the Center mix the Pole.
> Silence, ye troubl'd waves, and thou Deep, peace,
> Said then th' Omnific Word, your discord end:
> Nor staid, but on the Wings of Cherubim
> Uplifted, in Paternal Glorie rode
> Farr into *Chaos*, and the World unborn;
> For *Chaos* heard his voice: him all his Traine
> Follow'd in bright procession to behold
> Creation, and the wonders of his might.
> Then staid the fervid Wheeles, and in his hand
> He took the golden Compasses, prepar'd
> In Gods Eternal store, to circumscribe
> This Universe, and all created things:
> One foot he center'd, and the other turn'd
> Round through the vast profunditie obscure,
> And said, thus farr extend, thus farr thy bounds,
> This be thy just Circumference, O World.
> Thus God the Heav'n created, thus the Earth,
> Matter unform'd and void: Darkness profound
> Cover'd th' Abyss: but on the watrie calme
> His brooding wings the Spirit of God outspred,
> And vital vertue infus'd, and vital warmth

[1] For the possibility of Milton's deriving hints for his causeway from Philostratus's life of Apollonius see Appendix B (p. 171).

Throughout the fluid Mass, but downward purg'd
The black tartareous cold Infernal dregs
Adverse to life: then founded, then conglob'd
Like things to like, the rest to several place
Disparted, and between spun out the Air,
And Earth self ballanc't on her Center hung.

There are many comparisons and contrasts between the two creative acts; and one account helps to make the other more precise. The divine Trinity is matched by the infernal trinity of Satan, Sin, and Death; and it is the second and third in each trinity who execute the creative work. God hushes chaos into peace before creation, Sin and Death prefer to create from discordant material. The Holy Spirit broods like a dove over the abyss, Sin and Death hover over it like birds of prey. The spirit creates through warmth and growth and purges away the intractable dregs. Death solidifies his causeway by chill and petrifaction, and the solid and slimy materials he uses are doubtless those very 'cold infernal dregs, adverse to life' which the Spirit had rejected. Generally, the second passage is violent and excessive where the first passage is easy, though vast, and serene. And this excess co-operates with the parody in creating the sense of the grotesque. Death, 'the grim Feature', is so vaguely circumstantiated that we are all free to have our own picture of him, but, whatever the picture generally, it becomes grotesque when he 'upturns his Nostril wide into the murkie Air'. The mountains of ice piled up by by polar winds cannot be pictured otherwise than as grotesquely huddled together.

I have dwelt on the nature of the passage describing how Sin and Death built their causeway because that nature is so important to the structure of the whole book. It is Milton's first stroke in creating an impression of threatening monstrosity.

When Sin and Death have done their work, they arrive at the upper end of the causeway: that fateful road-junction on the zenith of the universe, where there is access at choice to Heaven or Hell or Earth. There, very dramatically, they meet Satan, and in the conversations that follow the setting should be remembered. When Sin, addressing her parent Satan, tells him that God may

> henceforth Monarchie with thee divide
> Of all things parted by th'Empyreal bounds,
> His Quadrature, from thy Orbicular World,

we should picture the trio standing on the outer shell of the 'Orbicular World' with a clear view down into its recesses and with God's 'Quadrature', the 'Opal Towrs and Battlements adorn'd of living saphire' seen by Satan when emerging from chaos, in distant prospect. Further, when Satan begins his injunctions with 'You two this way . . .' he should be pictured as pointing the way he has just come from Paradise. Once more the vast, circumstantiated picture is organic to the total impression required.

The trio now part, Sin and Death earthwards and Satan back to Hell to announce his good news. He finds Hell a strange sight, with the gate wide and unguarded, the outskirts deserted, and only the citadel, Pandemonium, in use. With the dictator's flair for the theatrical he steps through the devils assembled in the great hall, in lowly disguise, and appears suddenly to the company, seated in full splendour on the throne. There is no need to stress the grotesqueness of the sequel—for it is well recognized—Satan's boastful speech followed by the elaborate symbolic *tour de force* of the devils turned to serpents and vainly seeking to slake their thirst on the ashen fruit.[1] It is doubtful whether Milton was wise to assert just then, even if in oblique, symbolic form, that Satan's apparent triumph was illusory. And assert he does because he contrasts man's single lapse with the serpents' repeatedly tasting their own illusive fruit:

> so oft they fell
> Into the same illusion, not as Man
> Whom they triumph'd once lapst.

But this assertion counts little compared with Milton's success

[1] Waldock (*op. cit.*), 91, observes that Milton's technique in this scene is that of the comic cartoon. True, and in its setting it is none the worse for that.

in intensifying the grotesqueness, the monstrosity he has already created. By inserting the queer legend of Ophion and Eurynome, whom he equates with the Serpent and Eve—a strained bit of academicism in keeping just because it is strained—Milton makes a transition from Hell to Earth and the havoc now being worked there.

Sin and Death now arrive in Paradise and begin their work. They do not know that God is watching them and using them for his own purposes. In fact God proceeds to co-operate with them by sending his angels to shift the earth's angle so that the seasons may become less equable and generally to make life on earth harder and more subject to mutability. This is the third great account in Book Ten of evil or disorder gaining the mastery. The effects of the Fall are swelling to vast proportions. And this time they visibly affect man. There is the same effect as before of monstrous happenings. God does not just command, that things may happen easily and directly: he works through his angels, and they work laboriously, even doubtfully:

> Some say he bid his Angels turne ascanse
> The Poles of Earth twice ten degrees and more
> From the Suns Axle; they with labour push'd
> Oblique the Centric Globe; (x, 668.)

and Milton piles up the astronomical detail. Finally the eating of the forbidden fruit is compared to the fatal and unnatural feast of Thyestes with all its monstrous associations:

> At that tasted Fruit
> The Sun, as from Thyestean Banquet, turn'd
> His course intended.

Discord settles finally in Eden itself, where

> Beast now with Beast gan war, and Fowle with Fowle,
> And Fish with Fish; to graze the Herb all leaving,
> Devourd each other; nor stood much in awe
> Of Man.

The chaos caused by the Fall now fittingly culminates in the mind of man. It had been shown in Hell, when the devils become serpents, and in the natural world, and now at last it invades the human microcosm. Adam, observing the growing miseries around him, falls into sheer despair and utters a great tortured speech. He has changed greatly since his dumb self-centredness before the judging God. Then his mind was stupefied; now it works with terrifying speed and appears to take everything into account. The subject of the speech is justice self-applied. Adam seeks one excuse for his conduct after another and finds that every one fails. He then seeks one escape after another and finds each closed. Worst of all, the effects of his crime are not confined to himself but will be handed on to his posterity. He ends in unmitigated self-accusation:

> Him after all Disputes
> Forc't I absolve: all my evasion vain,
> And reasonings, though through Mazes lead me still
> But to my own conviction: first and last
> On mee, mee only, as the sourse and spring
> Of all corruption, all the blame lights due.

And he concludes that as his crime was simply that of Satan, so must his doom be likewise.[1]

To match Adam's despair we should go to *Samson Agonistes*; and for more than one reason. Adam and Samson both suffer so terribly because they can see no possible course of action; and they are both unaware that because they have searched their hearts to the bottom and really know themselves and admit every scruple of guilt they are even now saved men. And that is one of the many ironies into which the tenth book of *Paradise Lost* issues. You can put it another way by saying that in this place, where the processes of destruction and disorder appear to culminate, the process of regeneration has actually begun.

But it is only with a fraction of our mind that we apprehend the irony; with most of it we witness Adam's despair, and, in

---

[1] As we read this speech we are meant to recall Satan's great speech on Mount Niphates at the beginning of Book Four. Both speakers are tortured, both admit God's justice. But Satan ends in a resolve to do evil, Adam in self-accusation.

its vastness and complications, associate it with the vast grotesquenesses which have led up to it.

As Adam lies sleepless with these thoughts he makes a second and very different speech. It is short and though it is despairing in content it differs in tone from the storminess of the previous speech.

> Why comes not Death,
> Said hee, with one thrice acceptable stroke
> To end me? Shall Truth fail to keep her word,
> Justice Divine not hast'n to be just?
> But Death comes not at call, Justice Divine
> Mends not her slowest pace for prayers or cries.
> O Woods, O Fountains, Hillocks, Dales and Bowrs,
> With other echo late I taught your Shades
> To answer, and resound farr other Song.

It is not the terrible despair that here strikes us so much as the lyrical beauty. The Rev Dr Newton, whose sumptuous edition of *Paradise Lost* appeared in 1749 well in the middle of the age of reason, a man not given to excessive enthusiasm, in comment on the words,

> Justice Divine
> Mends not her slowest pace for prayers or cries,

(having duly noted an imitation of *Pede Poena claudo*, Hor. *Od.* III. ii. 32), wrote

> The most beautiful passages commonly want the fewest notes: And, for the beauties of this passage, we are sure, the reader must not only perceive, but really feel, them, if he has any feeling at all. Nothing in all the ancient tragedies is more moving and pathetick.

And it is pleasant to be able to record independent agreement with this editor on this singular beauty. But the beauty has a function. It hints that Adam, without knowing it (as the Ancient Mariner blessed the water-snakes unawares), is beginning a little to relax his mind's tension; and it prepares for the approach of Eve, who now begins to make up to him. But even here, Hell has not yet quite done its worst, and Adam rejects her with bitter words to herself and bitter words about sex in general. Chaos has invaded not only the single mind but the bonds between man and wife. I have changed my opinion about Adam's famous words on the misfortunes of marriage. Speaking of the husband Milton says

> for either
> He never shall find out fit Mate, but such
> As some misfortune brings him, or mistake,
> Or whom he wishes most shall seldom gain
> Through her perverseness, but shall see her gain'd
> By a farr worse, or if she love, witheld
> By Parents, or his happierr choice too late
> Shall meet, alreadie linkt and Wedlock-bound
> To a fell Adversarie, his hate and shame:
> Which infinite calamitie shall cause
> To Human life, and household peace confound.

I now agree with Hanford,[1] and disagree with Walter Raleigh in thinking these lines appropriately dramatic and not a piece of extrinsic comment on Milton's experience of marriage. Adam has already been deeply concerned with his posterity and now lets his imagination dwell on what it will suffer in the matter of wedlock through his own disobedience. His bitterness towards Eve is ferocious. The worse cut of all is when he accuses her of 'longing to be seen though by the Devil himself'. But I fancy the bitterness is mixed: part sheer resentment, part fury in recognizing that he is, after all, still drawn towards her. Compare Hamlet's brutality to Ophelia.

And now at last, following on the significant word 'confound', which ended the last quotation, comes the resolution, the act to which all the accumulation of incident and description recorded in this essay leads up: the reconciliation of Adam and Eve. It begins with Eve's persistence:

> He added not, and from her turn'd, but *Eve*
> Not so repulst, with Tears that ceas'd not flowing,
> And tresses all disordered, at his feet
> Fell humble, and imbracing them, besaught
> His peace.

[1] *Studies in Philology*, (1917), 186, from an article on 'The Dramatic Element in *Paradise Lost*'.

The lines are few and simple and yet charged with meaning. There is the fitness, indeed the artistic necessity, that as Eve took the initiative in sin she should take the initiative in regeneration. And there is the exquisite irony that her noble action should follow close upon Adam's fierce denunciation of her sex. And her action, however simple and simply described ('not so repulst'), is a sublime display of courage, involving the terrible pain of making the first motion, of breaking free from the deadly sin of Sloth. And in the scheme of the whole poem it is crucial: the first motion of sincere, positive, good feeling after all the falseness and frustration that has followed the Fall.

Eve's conciliatory speech follows. She too has no hope, and death may come in a few hours. She has no pride and is utterly open about her own fault. Indeed she wants to take all the blame on herself. But death or no death, she knows that for Adam and herself to be at odds is intolerable, and her resolution is equal to her humility. The union of these two qualities is irresistible, and Adam's hardness both towards her and towards heaven is melted. Here, if anywhere, is the crisis of *Paradise Lost*.

> She ended weeping, and her lowlie plight,
> Immoveable till peace obtain'd from fault
> Acknowledg'd and deplor'd, in *Adam* wrought
> Commiseration; soon his heart relented
> Towards her, his life so late and sole delight,
> Now at his feet submissive in distress,
> Creature so faire his reconcilement seeking,
> His counsel whom she had displeas'd, his aide;
> As one disarm'd, his anger all he lost,
> And thus with peaceful words uprais'd her soon.
>   Unwarie, and too desirous, as before,
> So now of what thou knowst not, who desir'st
> The punishment all on thy self; alas,
> Beare thine own first, ill able to sustaine
> His full wrauth whose thou feels't as yet lest part,
> And my displeasure bearst so ill. If Prayers
> Could alter high Decrees, I to that place
> Would speed before thee, and be louder heard,

That on my head all might be visited,
Thy frailtie and infirmer sex forgiv'n,
To me committed and by me expos'd.
But rise, let us no more contend, nor blame
Each other, blam'd enough elsewhere, but strive
In offices of Love, how we may light'n
Each others burden in our share of woe;
Since this days Death denounc't, if ought I see,
Will prove no sudden, but a slow-pac't evil,
A long day's dying to augment our paine,
And to our Seed (O hapless Seed) deriv'd.

In this speech Adam joins Eve in showing the first positive good feelings since the Fall. He pities Eve, he humbly admits his sin in allowing her to be exposed alone to temptation (an admission that was absent from his self-judgment in his tortured soliloquy), and he is courageous in facing the conditions of life and accepting the harsh fact that prayers cannot alter high decrees. And above all he has found the first outlet in action: they must 'strive in offices of Love' and seek to ease each other's burden.

But complete humility before God has not yet been reached. Eve still wants to deny the initiative to God. She, the practical one, has been thinking while Adam has been torturing himself with the metaphysics of justice. And she sees two ways out of their worst trouble, the incrimination of their posterity: namely, birth-control by abstinence, and suicide. Nowhere does Eve's quickness of apprehension come out better than in this speech. It is a model of lucid, practical reasoning. And she means what she says. But her mind is still in the grip of violent passion and—

She ended here, or vehement despaire
Broke off the rest; so much of Death her thoughts
Had entertained, as di'd her cheeks with pale.
But *Adam*, with such counsel nothing sway'd,
To better hopes his more attentive minde
Labouring had rais'd.

His more attentive minde: that is important, for in the speech that follows Adam recollects God's words and mien in giving judgment, hitherto lying dormant within him and quite over-laid by his own self-accusations. Adam also sees that Eve's proposals, though they argue the nobility of her nature, do imply acts of contumacy, aimed at defeating God's purposes. And God will not be cheated so easily. The Robinson Crusoe in Adam next begins to show itself, and he begins to have ideas about how life after the Fall can be lived. Hope has been born. But the only real cure is submission and penitence:

> What better can we do, then to the place
> Repairing where he judg'd us, prostrate fall
> Before him reverent, and there confess
> Humbly our faults, and pardon beg, with tears
> Watering the ground, and with our sighs the Air
> Frequenting, sent from hearts contrite, in sign
> Of sorrow unfeign'd, and humiliation meek,
> Undoubtedly he will relent and turn
> From his displeasure; in whose look serene,
> When angry most he seem'd and most severe
> What else but favour, grace, and mercie shone?

What had been latent in Adam's mind has now fully shown itself; and the rigorous justice by which he condemned his own acts is now consciously tempered by the mercy which he remembers God to have shown in the very act of pronouncing judgment.

Eve joins Adam in remorse, and the present phase of the action, so long sustained, at last comes to rest in Adam and Eve repairing to the place of judgment and imploring God's pardon.

Such are the details of the reconciliation and the penitence of Adam and Eve. It remains to say something of these things in the structure of the poem. For all the importance of the penitence, it is on the reconciliation that the fullest structural emphasis falls: in it Milton seems to have centred the most intimate significance of his poem. He has, in the actual poem, in his manipulation of his poetic material, carefully led every-thing up to this reconciliation. He had motivated the Fall with cunning skill, but not allowed us to dwell on it too long and too earnestly. Without pause he had widened the action from the bounds of Paradise. He had built up monstrous and grotesque pictures of chaos, while delicately insinuating the possibility of regeneration. And what issues out of it all? Something that initially looks like bathos: two ordinary human beings in despair, divided, and then coming together in ordinary human decency. The whole elaborate edifice has been staged to give all possible weight to a quite uncomplicated and commonplace trickle of pure human sympathy, the first touch of regeneration, a small beginning but stronger than all the pretensions of Satanic ingenuity, like some faint flow of pale, clear oil issuing from a huge and grotesquely carved oil-press: all this complication of apparatus just for *that*.

Looked at closer the human story of Adam and Eve's reconciliation is not bathos at all. First, it serves and crowns Milton's largest and most elaborate irony. According to Satan's plans the culmination of the story should have been the disobedient act and its dreadful consequences on earth and for its perpetrators. And these plans succeeded well enough in appearance to deceive Satan and Professor Raleigh. Now to the imagination of the Satan who stages so sensational a return to his fellows to report his success any retribution he feared for his daring would present itself in sensational terms. The war in heaven had been violent and noisy; and so had been the Son's entry to end the war in heaven:

> Forth rush'd with whirlwind sound
> The Chariot of Paternal Deitie.

Satan could recognize God in the whirlwind but not in the still small voice. And that God's retaliation could consist in evoking a simple effusion of decent human feeling out of the chaos he had created was beyond the grasp of his mind. And that all his strivings should have been the occasion of something so seemingly petty was a bitter piece of irony at his expense. So it is that the great and dreadful things that appear to be the most important subordinate themselves to what appears to be trivial and is yet surpassingly strong. And this is the essence of the way the nodal episode of *Paradise Lost* is plotted.

Secondly, Adam and Eve exemplify unconsciously in their acts the doctrine which Adam, instructed by the pageant of human history, pronounces in his last words to Michael near the end of the poem. Again it is ironical and perfectly true to life that the pair, while they are in the thick of action, do not know the full import of what they do, and that Adam has to be instructed from without before he can consciously formulate the principle on which he has already acted. Adam's comment on world-history and Michael's reply are poetry whose subdued tone is in inverse proportion to the passion of conviction that inspires it, and stand in the same relation to the great reverberant speeches of Satan in Book One as the episode of Adam's reconciliation with Eve stands to the monstrous events leading up to it. When Adam says,

> Henceforth I learne, that to obey is best,
> And love with fear the only God, to walk
> As in his presence, ever to observe
> His providence, and on him sole depend,
> Mercifull over all his works, with good
> Still overcoming evil, and by small
> Accomplishing great things, by things deemd weak
> Subverting worldly strong, and worldly wise
> By simply meek,

he might be describing his own and Eve's acts: their 'small' act of reconciliation 'accomplishing great things', their 'weak' prostration before God 'subverting' the 'worldly strong' of Satan, and their acceptance of the facts of their case constituting true obedience.

If I am right in thinking Books Nine and Ten inseparable, jointly the culminating area of the poem, and in seeing the Fall itself as the apparent, and the reconciliation of Adam and Eve as the real crisis, how does this affect the other parts of the poem? Such an alteration of balance cannot but make itself felt. I can see its effect on four main parts: the plot, the hero, Satan, and Milton's religion.

In the fifth chapter of the third part of my *Milton* I discussed the question whether there was any inconsistency between Milton's ideas about action as expressed first through Satan and secondly through the conduct of Adam and Eve leading to the Fall. It seemed important, because if Satan's journeys and the disobedience of Adam and Eve—the main active episodes, as I thought—should point different ways, the unity of the poem would suffer greatly. And I concluded that though Satan's journeys best expressed Milton's belief in heroic energy, the condemnation of triviality implicit in his version of the Fall was quite in keeping. Satan indeed gave the positive version, Adam and Eve the negative or oblique. But my argument was based on the false premise that the most significant acts of Adam and Eve could only be those leading up to their first disobedience. Since the centre of importance should be shifted to their regenerate action after the Fall, I was making a false comparison and a part of my chapter is null and void.

The stories of the two revolts, Satan's and Adam and Eve's, fall naturally into two parts: the motives prompting revolt, and the positive lines of action afterwards. And, just as naturally, when the critics compared the motives of the human pair with the subsequent action of the fallen angel they got wrong results. Let us see what happens when we make the natural comparisons: motive with motive, and action with action. Milton indeed invites us to do so. As to motives, the words of God the Father in Book Three (line 129) make the comparison:

> The first sort by their own suggestion fell,
> Self-tempted, self-deprav'd: Man falls deceiv'd
> By the other first: Man therefore shall find grace,
> The other none.

As to action, I have already pointed out how Adam's words to Michael near the end of the poem about overcoming 'worldly strong' by things thought weak do in fact refer to the deeds of Satan on the one hand and those of Adam and Eve on the other. If Milton himself drew these comparisons he meant us to heed and reflect on them. I will consider each in turn.

Of the two terms of the first comparison the motives of Adam and Eve for disobeying are far more fully described by

Milton and have been lavishly discussed by the critics. Satan's motives are briefly described and have been largely neglected. By referring to the human disobedience we may be able to learn something about the nature of the angelic. Adam and Eve fell for a variety of reasons, of which pride was one. Satan fell simply for an imagined insult to his pride; and there is no ground for arguing back from Adam and Eve in favour of a complication of motives in Satan. Pride, pure and simple, was the single and sufficient motive. But antecedent to each motive or set of motives was a single divine command. For Adam the command was a prohibition to eat the fruit; and however many other notions were associated with it, an arbitrary element was essential. Part of the point was that Adam and Eve should be kept in the dark, that just here their obedience should be unquestioning. It is from this necessarily arbitrary element in the prohibition that we can profitably argue back concerning the divine command that occasioned the disobedience of Satan. In Book Five Raphael recounts to Adam how, on a day when the angels were all still virtuous and before the universe was created, God summoned the whole host of heaven—plainly an occasion of the first moment—and made them this short and emphatic speech (line 600):

> Hear all ye Angels, Progenie of Light,
> Thrones, Dominations, Princedoms, Vertues, Powers,
> Hear my decree, which unrevoked shall stand,
> This day I have begot whom I declare
> My only Son, and on this holy Hill
> Him have anointed, whom ye now behold
> At my right hand; your Head I him appoint;
> And by my Self have sworn to him shall bow
> All knees in Heav'n, and shall confess him Lord;
> Under his great Vice-gerent Reign abide
> United as one individual Soule
> For ever happie: him who disobeys
> Mee disobeyes, breaks union, and that day
> Cast out from God and blessed vision, falls
> Into utter darkness, deep ingulft, his place
> Ordaind without redemption, without end.

If elsewhere God the Father speaks like a school divine, profuse of argument and explanation, he speaks here like a despot in curt harsh tones, commanding something about which no argument can be permitted. And I believe that no speech of God the Father has done so much to discredit Milton's representation of him as this one. But there is quite a simple explanation of why God adopts such a harsh tone. Bearing in mind the arbitrary prohibition to eat the fruit, we should see that God in this speech is presenting to the angels precisely the same test as later he presented to Adam and Eve. Thus a chief point of the command to the angels to worship the Son as their head was that they should have no immediate[1] notion why it was given. And if instead of being cryptic and terse God had apologized at length for not being able to give explicit reasons, the test would have been the less searching.

That Milton meant God to speak severely here is further shown by the parallel passage where God first informs Adam of his prohibition. This was conveyed to Adam not through an angelic medium but by God direct; and the exact terms of its conveyance are news to Raphael, to whom Adam narrates it:

> But of the Tree whose operation brings
> Knowledge of good and ill, which I have set
> The Pledge of thy Obedience and thy Faith,
> Amid the Garden by the Tree of Life,
> Remember what I warne thee, shun to taste,
> And shun the bitter consequence: for know,
> The day thou eat'st thereof, my sole command
> Transgrest, inevitably thou shalt dye;
> From that day mortal, and this happie State
> Shalt loose, expelld from hence into a World
> Of woe and sorrow. Sternly he pronounc'd
> The rigid interdiction, which resounds
> Yet dreadful in mine eare. (VIII, 323.)

[1] It is true that Abdiel (vi, 826–7) conjectures that through the Son's appointment as their head, the state of the angels may become in some way more exalted as better unified. But it is conjecture, and his main argument against Satan's rebellion is the outrage of the creature questioning the wisdom of the creator.

There is no postscript to God's speech to the Angels, to correspond to the last sentence. Nor is any needed, for the speech succeeds in conveying its own rigorous tone.

Both tests proceed quite naturally from the hierarchical ideas on which Milton's thought was grounded. To a certain hierarchical grade a certain degree of knowledge was appropriate. One side of obedience was not to aspire beyond it. This is a recurrent theme in *Paradise Lost*, culminating in Adam's words to Michael near the end of the poem when he has finished seeing the pageant of history:

> Greatly instructed I shall hence depart,
> Greatly in peace of thought, and have my fill
> Of knowledge, what this Vessel can containe;
> Beyond which was my folly to aspire.

Now it is impossible to exercise free obedience to the principle of limiting knowledge to your capacity, unless you are made aware of there being knowledge beyond your capacity and are given the chance of seeking to attain it or at least of challenging the fact. Satan, given a command beyond the capacity of even an archangel to understand, refuses to admit to a capacity inferior to the divine; Adam and Eve, forbidden for no given reason to eat the fruit, see in the fruit itself an extension of the knowledge suited to their condition and aspire through it to a place beyond that appointed to them in the total hierarchy.

Doctrinally, then, God's curt speech is reasonable, and being so should present fewer difficulties as poetry. But this is by the way. The main point is that the motives of Satan and of Adam and Eve to disobey are similarly grounded and that, far from there being any Satanic preponderance, the emphasis is strongly on the ultimately far more complicated motivation of the human pair.

We come now to the question of how the plot fares when we compare not, as on the old plan, the action leading to Eve's Fall, but the behaviour of Adam and Eve after it, with Satan's behaviour after his revolt.

Now the acts of Satan, as set forth in the poem, are divided into two. The immediate consequences of his revolt, his seducing a third of the angels, the war in Heaven, the fall into Hell, are narrated half-way through by Raphael, while only the acts after this fall are presented directly. Further, it is God himself and the good angels that Satan's early acts concern. The result is that though the battle in Heaven and Satan's fall do correspond to the ruin Adam and Eve bring on themselves and on nature by eating the fruit, we simply do not, in reading, make the comparison. The virtue of the human action is not drawn on to counterpoise the Satanic action, the necessary counterpoise being supplied by the hosts of Heaven. It is far otherwise with Satan's action at the opening of the poem. Heaven is then remote; Satan's feelings are human feelings; the infernal council is a humanly political debate: and inevitably we compare the infernal action in and beyond Hell with the human action in Paradise.

The main point therefore now is whether in actual fact, as we read, the reconciliation of Adam and Eve and their repentance before God have sufficient weight in the poem to balance the grandeur of Satan and his doings in the first books. By themselves, through mere lack of bulk, they hardly could. But they are, through Milton's art, inseparable from the huge and monstrous and ironical events out of which they issue and borrow from them a grandeur to which in their bare selves they could hardly pretend. Moreover they lead in Book Eleven to a scene in Heaven and to the representation in world history of the lessons which in a smaller way they themselves illustrated. From all this it follows that the crisis, as now conceived, in no way lets us down as the mere action of the Fall did. Nevertheless, some readers will probably go on thinking that there is nothing that quite equals the poetic fire with which Satan and his deeds are described early in the poem. If they are right, then they may follow Waldock[1] in thinking not that Milton was on the devil's side without knowing it but that he had at all costs to make his narrative initially interesting, that if Satan got just a little too big for Milton's

[1] 66–7.

plans it was through a poetic necessity and not through a relaxation of the Freudian censor.

Turning to the hero, I begin with the assumption that Adam, or Adam and Eve, are hero and that there are close analogies between *Paradise Lost* and the medieval theme of *Everyman*. The whole trend of the plot and of the geography make Adam and Eve central; and Heaven and Hell fight for them. To make Christ, the most active heavenly agent, the hero would be as wrong as to make God the hero of *Everyman*. One reason for the heresy that Satan is the hero is that on the old interpretation of the crisis Adam had no power of positive action: resistance to Satan was the best that was open to him; he could not even carry the war into Satan's own country and try to win him back to God, for Satan was inconvertible. Put the crisis at the reconciliation and the repentance, and positive action can and does take place. And Milton deliberately pits the actions of Adam and Eve against those of Satan, considering them more truly heroic. The gain is very great. Instead of regretting how little chance of heroism mankind had in prelapsarian Paradise we can now appreciate the pair's heroic self-extrication from the slough of inertia, comparable with Satan's self-elevation from the burning lake. Only Adam rises to labour well, Satan to procure ill. Adam shows heroic courage in facing and making the best of God's curse on him:

> On me the Curse aslope
> Glanc'd on the ground, with labour I must earne
> My bread; what harm? Idleness had bin worse;
> My labour will sustain me; and least Cold
> Or Heat should injure us, his timely care
> Hath unbesought provided, and his hands
> Cloath'd us unworthie, pitying while he judg'd.

Adam here shows that 'better fortitude of patience' which in the prologue to Book Nine Milton set against the inferior fortitude of the conventional epic hero.

Not that Adam is only the patient hero, for he goes on to show what I called the Robinson Crusoe in him. The growing inclemency of the elements

> bids us seek
> Some better shroud, some better warmth to cherish
> Our Limbs benumm'd; ere this diurnal Starr
> Leave cold the Night, how we his gather'd beams
> Reflected, may with matter sere foment,
> Or by collision of two bodies grinde
> The Air attrite to Fire.

No, Adam is still the active hero: the substitute of the Arthur (or of the later Alfred) who was to have been the hero of the earlier projected epic.

So long as the crisis was centred on the Fall and Adam was thus denied all power of positive action, Satan could with some plausibility be made the hero. Adam and Eve, it could be argued, are so insignificant that Satan is the best of the three, deserves the success his superior initiative brought, and had Milton's real if unacknowledged sympathy. Nothing of the kind can be maintained when the chief point of the crisis is the delusion of Satan and the ironic defeat of his apparently gigantic efforts by the small decencies of the human pair. You might as well argue that the author of the Book of Samuel was really on the side of Goliath against David. That Milton either consciously or unconsciously thought Satan the hero in the culminating books is now more than ever out of the question.

What applies to Satan, applies, with due modifications, to Milton's religion. More than ever is it certain that Milton was on the side of Christian humility against pride. It is, one hopes, fully recognized by now that in the last conversation between Michael and Adam near the end of the poem Milton stated the doctrine of Christian humility with incomparable passion and force. But that force is vastly increased when it is seen that the true crisis of *Paradise Lost* was a dramatic presentation of that very doctrine, rendered all the weightier through the irony of the actors not realizing what high principle their deeds were in fact setting forth.

These, then, are some of the ways in which the adjustment of balance I have advocated affects *Paradise Lost*. What is the general conclusion? Simply that there is no major flaw in the poem. There may be this or that detail which this or that reader dislikes: the presentation of God the Father, for instance. But this is still but a detail and counts for little compared with a weakness in the part of the poem where strength is most needed. If, as I argue, such a weakness is imaginary, any deficiency in the poem will simply be the inevitable limitations of a human being, the poet; and to describe it will mean no more than to say that Milton cannot do certain things which Virgil or Dante, for instance, can do. In *Paradise Lost* Milton expressed, as fully as a human artist can, the range of what he was good for.

A Note on Satan

SINCE writing my *Milton* I have slightly altered my conception of Satan. Of this altered conception there are hints
in the two last sections. This note expands those hints to a
length that would not have been suitable in their context.

There are reasons why we are in a better position than we
were thirty or even twenty years ago to get a true picture of
Milton's Satan. Scholars have taught us more about Milton's
theology; events have robbed the act of rebellion of
the romance it enjoyed in more tranquil days and have
forced upon us a new knowledge of the dictator-type. Even
those readers who insist on finding an arbitrary element in
Milton's God must admit that Milton also pictured him as
that to which the whole natural order led up; and if they conceive of Satan as defying a tyrant they cannot escape con-
ceiving of him as opposing the whole natural order too. Such
a mixed opposition makes him much less purely romantic
than did, as once pictured, his lonely defiance of a powerful
potentate. But even if we *could* legitimately retain this picture
we should today get less pleasure in doing so. Opposition,
intransigeance, rebellion, assertion of personal rights at all
costs—these are matters we have seen too much of, and we
are correspondingly more friendly to what used to be considered the Deadly Virtues. We begin with less prejudice in
favour of Satan, as rebel, than we once did. How our new
knowledge of dictator-type should help us with Satan I will
say later.

But if we can avoid more easily the danger of sentimentaliz-
ing the rebel, we expose ourselves to the opposite danger of
making him too cheap. And that is what Charles Williams[1]
and C. S. Lewis[2] have done. Briefly, they substitute a ridi-

[1] *The English Poems of Milton* (World's Classics, 1940), xiii–xvii.
[2] *A Preface to 'Paradise Lost'* (London, 1942), 92–100. For retorts to C. S.
Lewis see E. E. Stoll, *Give the Devil His Due* in *Review of English Studies*, 1944,
and G. Rostrevor Hamilton, *Hero or Fool?* (London, 1944)

culous for the old august figure. The key to Satan are the 'high disdain' and 'sense of injured merit' to which he himself admits in the first book of the poem: feelings which are at odds with the true facts and render the holder of them ridiculous. To this absurdity the laughter of Heaven is the appropriate answer. These opinions are specious because they are joined with others which are both true (and of a truth that needs emphatic assertion at the present time) and because they have some backing from Milton's text. Here is one of such true opinions, from Charles Williams's preface:

> Milton thought pride, egotism, and a proper sense of one's own rights the greatest of all temptations; he was, no doubt, like most people, subject to it. And he thought it led straight to inaccuracy and malice, and finally to idiocy and hell.

That is so true of Milton himself that we are tempted to accept the less critically Williams's neighbouring remarks about Satan. And we *should* take them critically, because though thay can (as I said) be substantiated by the literal text of *Paradise Lost* they cannot be by the poetry.

Let me examine the alleged absurdity of Satan. In my section on the *Crisis of Paradise Lost* I wrote of the great irony at Satan's expense, of the way his grandiose plans turned out differently from what he expected, and his big things were defeated by the small things of Adam and Eve. It is a vast irony and poetically it is absolutely appropriate to the vast figure Milton created of Satan at the beginning of the poem. The irony promotes feelings more akin to the tragic than to the absurd and in no way diminishes the stature of its victim. Nor do I disagree with Williams when he finds irony at Satan's expense from the very beginning. There Satan speaks of himself as

> one who brings
> A mind not to be chang'd by Place or Time.
> The mind is its own place, and in itself
> Can make a Heav'n of Hell, a Hell of Heav'n.

Here the irony is that Satan means these words and thinks them true in one way, while they are true only in another, hidden way. He means that the separated mind is its own master and can impose its own chosen feelings on any circumstances. It can make itself happy against any odds. But, unsuspected by Satan, it can mean that (as for Donne in Twickenham Garden) no propitiousness of time or place can help, that a mental hell will remain, whether in view of Paradise or in the courts of Heaven itself. And this is the true meaning as Satan was to learn and admit later. But once again absurdity is precluded through the splendour of the poetical context. Satan is too tremendous a figure here to be ridiculous, and we are no more inclined to laugh than when the Oedipus of Sophocles unwittingly invokes curses on his own head.

But there is one place where Milton seems to take sides against the effects which his poetry has undoubtedly produced or leads us to expect. Charles Williams noted it and used it to support his notion of Satan's absurdity. It is the place (v, 711) where God the Father noticed that Satan had withdrawn a third part of the angels with hostile intent,

> And smiling to his onely Son thus said,
> Son, thou in whom my glory I behold
> In full resplendence, Heir of all my might,
> Neerly it now concernes us to be sure
> Of our Omnipotence, and with what Arms
> We mean to hold what anciently we claim
> Of Deitie or Empire, such a foe
> Is rising, who intends to erect his Throne
> Equal to ours.

And the Son, in answering, says that the Father justly has his foes in derision. Here, plainly, Satan is *meant* to appear ridiculous. The Father is being highly ironical at Satan's expense in putting his own omnipotence in the terms of Satan's limited and distorted conception: that of an earthly monarch claiming his throne on ancient precedent. And considered in abstraction from the poetic context Satan *should* appear ridiculous. To defy omnipotence is silly, while the revolt of a third of Heaven's denizens is of no moment in the eyes of one who can replace them at will out of nothing. But such thoughts are far from the reader who bears the *total* poetic context in his mind. To him the defection of a third of Heaven and the diversion of so much energy to evil is tragic, and the laughter of God is in the worst of taste. We cannot share it, and can only think that the appropriate celestial feeling was not mirth but a kind of horrified grief. But there is no doubt that Milton fully intended God's humour here, because he had made him act in the same way before, and in a most emphatic place. In the very first words the Father speaks (iii, 80) he refers to Satan in the same ironical tone:

> Onely begotten Son, seest thou what rage
> Transports our adversarie, whom no bounds
> Prescrib'd, no barrs of Hell, nor all the chains
> Heapt on him there, nor yet the main Abyss
> Wide interrupt can hold; so bent he seems
> On desperat reveng.

Commenting on these lines Waldock charges Milton with gross and unpardonable inconsistency in forgetting that it was through the 'sufferance of supernal Power' that Satan rose from the fiery lake. But God was being ironical, not inconsistent. He was mocking Satan by uttering as if true the false suppositions of independence on which Satan was acting; he was doing just what he did when he told the Son that they must look out for their omnipotence. Yet here Milton does not commit an error of taste. The Father's whole speech refers to the total action and to the major irony that pervades it; and it does not violate the complex of feelings that the two first books have set up. Indeed, the reader has had sufficient of Hell's murk and is ready for the antithesis which God's lucid irony succeeds in proposing.

In the poem itself the absurdity of Satan, or rather the moments when absurdity is his prime attribute (a dram of absurdity is never absent), are confined to a single passage, and one with which the reader is forced to quarrel.

In mediating between the two extreme conceptions of Satan just outlined I arrive at the very obvious but sometimes forgotten observation that, as Milton initially presents him,

Satan is a certain kind of tragic figure. He is neither the hero with whom Milton in his heart morally sympathizes, the kin of Shelley's Prometheus, nor the fundamentally stupid and hence ridiculous rebel; but, as Milton himself calls him, a ruined archangel, a creature of the highest endowments perverted to ill. And such perversion is a terrible and tragic thing. Of course Satan was stupid, but it is terrible and tragic that one whose mental endowments were so transcendent should fall into stupidity; just as it is terrible and tragic that one whose capacity for love was so great should pervert that capacity to hate. It may be that if men were more like God and less like themselves they would find perverted greatness an object of derision, but as men they wonder at greatness of whatever kind even if they abhor it when perverted. And it is surely the quality of Milton's Satan that, like Macbeth, he inspires contrary feelings: the desire to approach and gaze because of his greatness, the desire to shrink and avoid because of his cruelty; the desire to approach and support because of his courage, the desire to flee because of the madness on which it is based. But Satan is a vaster and more comprehensive figure than Macbeth. Macbeth is the protagonist in a very great play; Satan is the classic embodiment of the eternal dictator-type. Macbeth goes down before the forces of good. So does Satan, yet he will reappear and fight the same hopeless nefarious fight through all time.

Such a conception of Satan is, in spite of the paradox it contains, plain and comprehensible enough. Yet that many people will find it difficult appears from the way they took the most eminent example of the dictator-type in recent years. Many of Hitler's admirers thought him a god, many of his enemies a vague monster. To think of him as a great man with a large capacity for good mainly diverted to evil was not so easy. Yet no man could have written the account in the second chapter of *Mein Kampf* of how a country lad can be corrupted by life in a big city unless capable of a warm human sympathy; and no subsequent misdeeds could alter that fact. The only proper disposition towards Hitler is mixed. There is another analogy. If we can trust the likenesses, there was an expression in Hitler's face that declared his knowledge of ultimate doom. Its obvious absence from the faces of his followers confirms its apparent presence in his. Now, after Satan's first speech of all, Milton describes him as 'vaunting aloud, but rackt with deep despare'; and it is precisely Satan's distinction and attraction (from which horror is not divided) that he does despair and that in spite of his despair he rises to a height of insensate courage.[1]

P. P. Morand[2] and Waldock[3] think Satan becomes a different character after the second book. I do not think it matters greatly if he does, because much happens between this book and Satan's self-revealing speech on Mount Niphates in Book Four, where he is said to show a change. We are not worried in any ordinary consecutive reading. But I doubt if any change need be posited, and rather agree with Rajan[4] that what side of his character Satan shows depends on the circumstances. If his lone awakening on the fiery lake evoked astonishing courage, the sight later on of so many legions assembled tempted him to a coarseness of pride:

> And now his heart
> Distends with pride, and hardning in his strength
> Glories: For never since created man,
> Met such imbodied force. . . . (i, 571–4.)

To command so many bred a kind of intoxication. And this mood continues in the opening of Book Two, where Satan appears seated on his throne 'and from despair thus high uplifted beyond hope'. He was more impressive in his despair and his action in spite of it. But on Niphates he lacks the support of his fellows, the soothing illusion of strength through mere numbers, and the pride of leadership. Moreover he has left his realm of darkness. He is alone and in the now alien realm of light. No wonder if he changes his tone. Claudius in *Hamlet* behaves in much the same way. He is confident and

---

[1] Waldock (78) sees a discrepancy between Satan's speech and Milton's gloss. He finds nothing despairing in the speech itself. But I remember nothing despairing in Gayda's articles shortly before the fall of Mussolini.

[2] *De Comus à Satan* (Paris, 1939), 140.

[3] 82.

[4] *Reader* (London, 1947), 96–104. *Paradise Lost and the Seventeenth Century.*

efficient and kingly in public (except at the crisis of the play-scene); left alone he shows a very different side of himself in his attempted prayers. Yet he is not usually considered an inconsistent character.

In my *Milton* (277) I wrote that I had to admit that 'Milton did partly ally himself with Satan, that unwittingly he was led away by the creature of his own imagination'. The first part of this statement is self-evident. We have all got Satan within us, and Milton to picture Satan convincingly had to ally himself partly with the Satan within himself. Whether in this process he went farther than he meant is another matter. That he went much farther is inconceivable. Ultimately Milton was a reasonable man who took life as it is. Nevertheless, he was sometimes possessed of an initial urge to force things to be other than they are. Wisdom in the end asserted itself, but it sometimes took Milton a little time to see where pride was leading him. In his early pamphleteering days he allowed his Utopian hopes more scope than a wise man should, though this did not ultimately prevent him from seeing that a change of church government need not imply a change of heart in the governed. Both Milton and his Satan suffered from the romantic complaint of the love of the impossible, and though in Milton that love may have been effectively checked and balanced it may have led him, in the heat of composition, to give to the same quality in Satan just a little more indulgence than he meant. It is foolish to expect utter perfection in a human artist. And if Milton's wisdom had asserted itself, when he created Satan, with a more rigid and speedy conscientiousness, he might have created a less exciting figure. I do not now think, granted Milton's ultimate wisdom, that the question whether he gave Satan a little more rope than he meant is very important. And it is always possible that the rather persistent idea that he did so can be a misstatement of the possibility (already mentioned) to which Waldock[1] pointed: that Milton, writing a narrative poem, had at all costs to secure the initial interest of his reader; beginning with Satan he had no option but to write him up.

[1] 66–7.

So far I have pleaded for the rightness of Satan as a poetic character. I will end by pointing to a difficulty in his character which I have not seen noticed before.

Milton could hardly do other than he did in making Satan a tragic and hence a mainly human figure and in giving his followers very human characteristics. His Hell, unlike Dante's, had no human inhabitants. To make it interesting Milton was forced in compensation to humanize his devils rather than to make them represent essential evil. How remote Satan is from essential evil can be seen if you compare him with Macbeth and Iago respectively. Plainly he resembles Macbeth and not Iago; and as plainly Iago is closer to essential evil than Macbeth. That is of course as it should be, for if Iago had been a character framed for great good and perverted to evil he would have been a tragic figure and have competed with Othello for the position of hero, to the great detriment of the play. Now Milton also wanted to convey a sense of essential evil and he chose to do so—and what else could he now do in view of what he had already created?—through Satan. He therefore turned Satan from a human into an allegorical figure and made him bear Sin out of his head as Zeus bore Athena or Wisdom. Then from his union with Sin was born Death. This allegory also serves a dominant motive throughout the poem: the parody by evil of the powers of Heaven.[1] It was noted (p. 32) how Sin and Death, in making their bridge, parodied divine creation. Now Satan, Sin, and Death are a close parody of the Trinity. Satan corresponds to the Father. He begets a daughter Sin, and proceeding from them both there is the third member of the infernal Trinity, Death.

It must be granted that Milton prepares for his allegory with very great skill. Such skill was needed, for the difficulties were great. If Satan in Book One is a tragic and hence a largely human figure, the devil-orators in Book Two are even more human. The humanizing process continues after the council is dissolved (506), when the devils turn to the pastimes that best suit their different temperaments. They create

[1] For a detailed account of the many correspondences in *Paradise Lost* see Rajan, 44ff.

a number of ways of life, and human at that, which are wrong only because they lack a foundation. In fact these are not ways of life but pastimes pursued to anaesthetize a fundamental misery. Milton is being strictly true to a sad side of ordinary human behaviour. But when (570) he describes another group of devils organizing an expedition of discovery that leads them to the geography of the classical Hades, he gives quite a new turn to his poem. Milton was passionately interested in contemporary travel and exploration, the overland trade-routes to India for instance, and his exploratory devils add yet another to the already described anaesthetizing pastimes; but the land they discover is quite remote from any life lived on this earth. It is an allegorical land whose geographical features, the infernal rivers, the Furies, and Medusa figure with terrible success a world of abstract and unformulated passions, the world of vague mental chaos which is the reality underlying the precise human occupations with which the devils have been trying to solace and drug themselves. It is a wonderful description and it serves to introduce Satan in his allegorical role of father of Sin and Death.

Now, to a generation of readers to whom Spenser was the chief English poetical classic, there would be little difficulty in allowing a very human figure to melt into allegory and then to reassume human form. But we have not been thus bred, and one of the most alien scenes for us in the poem is that before Hell Gate when Satan seeking a way out of Hell is confronted by his own daughter. We feel that things have been put the wrong way round. It is the abstraction that should come first, and from the abstraction should spring this and that embodiment. Satan should have been the child of Sin and Death not their parent. Luckily it is only here in the poem that the relationship is forced on us. Elsewhere we are mostly free to ignore it. How present is it in our minds, at the end of Book Four, for instance, when Satan, confronted with Gabriel and his angelic guard, sees himself wanting in God's balances, and turns in utter flight? Milton's imagination was able to triumph over the inconveniences to which it was sometimes committed.

Satan, Gabriel and the Plowman

I ENDED my note on Satan with a reference to the last lines of Book Four of *Paradise Lost*, where, I maintained, Milton's imagination was free to work. I should have liked to go farther and use the passage to illustrate what Milton really felt about Satan. But the passage is splendid in so many ways that it would have been difficult to use it to point one way only. I therefore give it a note to itself.

Here is the passage. It is Satan who has just spoken.

> While thus he spake, th'Angelic Squadron bright
> Turnd fierie red, sharpning in mooned hornes
> Thir Phalanx, and began to hemm him round
> With ported Spears, as thick as when a field   980
> Of *Ceres* ripe for harvest waving bends
> Her bearded Grove of ears, which way the wind
> Swayes them; the careful Plowman doubting stands
> Least on the threshing floore his hopeful sheaves
> Prove chaff. On th'other side *Satan* allarm'd
> Collecting all his might dilated stood,
> Like *Teneriff* or *Atlas* unremov'd:
> His stature reacht the Skie, and on his Crest
> Sat horror Plum'd; nor wanted in his graspe
> What seemd both Spear and Shield: now dreadful deeds   990
> Might have ensu'd, nor onely Paradise
> In this commotion, but the starrie Cope
> Of Heav'n perhaps, or all the Elements
> At least had gon to rack, disturbd and torne
> With violence of this conflict, had not soon
> Th'Eternal to prevent such horrid fray
> Hung forth in Heav'n his golden scales, yet seen
> Betwixt *Astraea* and the *Scorpion* signe,
> Wherein all things created first he weighd,
> The pendulous round Earth with ballanc't Aire   1000
> In counterpoise, now ponders all events,
> Battels and Realms: in these he put two weights
> The sequel each of parting and of fight;
> The latter quick up flew, and kickt the beam;
> Which *Gabriel* spying, thus bespake the Fiend.

Satan, I know thy strength, and thou knowst mine,
Neither our own but giv'n; what follie then
To boast what Arms can doe, since thine no more
Then Heav'n permits, nor mine, though doubld now
To trample thee as mire: for proof look up,   1010
And read thy Lot in yon celestial Sign
Where thou are weigh'd and shown how light, how weak,
If thou resist. The Fiend lookt up and knew
His mounted scale aloft: nor more; but fled
Murmuring, and with him fled the shades of night.

First, there are a few points of meaning on which one
should be clear. In 978 one should surely imagine a comma
between *turnd* and *fierie*. The angel guard, already fiery red,
turned their flanks inward. Many readers, I dare wager,
picture them as going red with rage; I cannot think they are
right, or even that we must accept a double meaning. Next,
we cannot appreciate the image of the corn unless we know
that in the *port* the spear was held diagonally across the body,
the pointed end reaching well above the head. In 985 *allarm'd*
does not mean *frightened* but *ready for action*, the military
sense. In 987 *unremov'd* means *not to be remov'd*. The scales
God lets down concern Satan alone. In them he puts the
weight or the advisability of what for Satan follows if he
should fly and if he should fight. Satan's capacity for battle
and hence the advisability of accepting it weighs less than the
advisability of flight. His strength has been weighed in the
balance and been found wanting. Looking up to Heaven he
knows it and can do only one thing.

The passage itself reminds me of the rock fragment
Whymper found on the summit of the Matterhorn at his first
ascent: a replica in miniature of the mountain itself. The
Plowman, though an apparently arbitrary extension of a
simile, is crucial. He comes between the description of the
angelic guard and that of Satan. Through this position he is
the focus of the powers of Heaven and Hell and thus resembles
Adam and Eve. Next, it hangs in the balance whether the
solid gain of corn or the chaos of chaff shall be the reward of
his labours. When Satan at the end flees murmuring, we know

that chaos will not prevail. The Plowman does something else. He attaches the gigantic play of the other actors to the homeliness of earth, as at the end of the poem the mist rising at the heel of the labourer returning home at evening corrects the otherwise overwhelming effect of the cherubim with their dreadful faces and fiery arms. Heaven, Hell, and the humblest and most quotidian of man's doings are not to be separated. The words *bearded Grove of ears* work the same way. *Grove* implies trees: thus within the simile we get another case of big and small things brought together. (*Bearded* is exquisitely apt in making the transition from grain-stalks to trees; the beards of the grain suggesting the leaves that would be on the trees in harvest-time.)

The two descriptions that flank the Plowman are equally rich in meaning. The angelic squadron are compared to a homely and multiple and miniature phenomenon, the stalks of a field of grain; Satan is compared to a vast, romantic, isolated phenomenon, a mountain, and not just to any mountain but either an island volcano or one which was said in mythology to uphold the vault of heaven. Thinking of the *Grove of Ears*, we conceive the notion of close solidity, *grove* suggesting a congregation and the ears suggesting the concentrated ripe grain within them. The angelic squadron, though unostentatious, though composed of angels of lower degree than Satan's, is solid and useful. It is because we retain this notion that the contrary notion in the word *dilated*, applied to Satan, is so gloriously apt. It is equally apt that the vague personification of Horror should sit on his crest and that his arms should be vague if gigantic appearances. Satan himself is such as I have tried to describe him in my *Note on Satan*. The odds are hopelessly against him, he is utterly outnumbered and Hell is far away. Yet his courage does not fail, and Milton pays tribute to it in the grandeur of the comparison. But our admiration for his courage is crossed by the horror and madness of it. Satan's *dilation* betrays an ultimate hollowness, and we know it can be no match for the solid and truthful grain of angelic obedience. Here, in anticipation of the crisis of the poem, is the master theme of:

> with good
> Still overcoming evil, and by small
> Accomplishing great things, by things deemd weak
> Subverting worldly strong, and worldly wise
> By simply meek.

The descriptions of the three parties—angelic, human, infernal—completed, the poet conjectures what would have happened if the impending battle had taken place; and in the conjecture of what havoc would have followed he echoes by implication the previous potential havoc of empty chaff beneath the thresher's flail. The elements would have slipped back to chaos, as barren and wild as the flying chaff in the threshing shed. But this, God's providence will not allow; and just as later the rainbow was to signify the end of destruction by flood, so now the heavenly sign of the Scales, then first revealed to sight, signifies the heavenly decree of justice and the eternal stability of the heavens. The complex of references, biblical and classical, clustering round these heavenly scales can be learnt from any competent annotated edition of *Paradise Lost*, but surely they are subordinate to these great overriding ideas of God asserting his justice and the triumph of order over disorder, of the chain of being over chaos.

It is highly significant that Gabriel sees the new heavenly sign before Satan. Unfallen, he has the quicker apprehension. The brevity and simplicity of his speech are the perfect mirror of what he and his guard stand for; absolute humility joined with absolute assurance. And yet in

> though doubld now
> To trample thee as mire

Gabriel touches a height of passion not to be surpassed in poetry. Further, the speech is essentially (though not in any crude or offensive way) Protestant, in that it expresses that luminous sense of uninterrupted intercourse between creator and creature which though not in the least an exclusively Protestant doctrine was nevertheless the peculiar attribute of the highest Protestant vision. It is because Gabriel draws his strength without medium or obstruction from God that he knows in an instant that his strength is doubled and that in this inspired state he can trample Satan, his naturally stronger, like mire.

Satan's brief flight is definitive. The single adjective *murmuring* suffices to tell his disintegration. Rhetoric, threats, even words have broken down into feeble, inarticulate noise. And in its flight the mountain-like figure is swallowed up in the greater darkness of night now symbolically replaced by the light, the first offspring of Heaven.

In comparing the whole passage to the miniature of the Matterhorn I may not have been quite accurate, unless the miniature was a little more fairly proportioned than the original; for the passage succeeds in just those matters where the total poem is apt to go wrong. Unhampered by his certain allegiance to *Genesis* and by his possible allegiance to the tradition of the Miracle Plays, Milton can describe God through his attributes and his works and not in person. The effect is prodigious. Satan was vast, the heavenly Scales vaster by far, and they merely hint at that infinity that can only preserve dignity and escape bathos if left to the imagination. With Satan, Milton succeeds equally. Instead of begetting a symbolic figure, Satan is absorbed into a symbolic darkness vaster than himself. And that is the right way round.

Of the imagination that fused in a single unit of poetry the homely Plowman worried over the harvest and the monstrous figure of the golden Scales it is impossible to speak. Nor do I believe Milton could have spoken. The elements of his poetry he had amassed and then winnowed and sifted with the ferocity of a passionate nature and with the conscientiousness of a Puritan; but the gift that chose just those elements and put them together in just those proportions was a mystery, coming from what he called his

> Celestial Patroness, who deignes
> Her nightly visitation unimplor'd,
> And dictates to me slumbring, or inspires
> Easie my unpremeditated Verse.

Adam and Eve in Paradise

TO make fun of the life Adam and Eve led in Paradise is an easy game; and it is one I have to admit having played. But it is usually played on the wrong premise, namely that Milton pictured this life as perfect and fully developed, and that it would have continued for ever, had the pair kept God's command.

Now this premise, as Diekhoff[1] pointed out in a very interesting argument on the *felix culpa*, goes clean contrary to Milton's text. When the Father, after the rebel angels' defeat, declares to the assembly of heavenly powers his intention to create a new world with a new race from which to fill the gaps in the angelic ranks, he sketches out what should be the process of replenishment. And that process is not through a fall and a redemption but through a ripening of unfallen powers. God says he

> will create
> Another world, out of one man a Race
> Of men innumerable, there to dwell,
> Not here, till by degrees of merit rais'd
> They open to themselves at length the way
> Up hither, under long obedience tri'd,
> And Earth be chang'd to Heav'n, and Heav'n to Earth,
> One Kingdom, Joy and Union without end. (vii, 154–161.)

Earlier in the poem, though later in the action, Raphael, in his first and most important homiletic speech to Adam and Eve (v, 469–505), said the same. After describing how the higher reaches of the scale of being grow out of the lower, he says that man, if he remains obedient, may follow the same process and end by reaching the angelic state:

> Your bodies may at last turn all to Spirit,
> Improv'd by tract of time, and wingd ascend

[1] John S. Diekhoff, *Milton's Paradise Lost* (New York, 1946), 126–32.

> Ethereal, as we, or may at choice
> Here or in Heavn'ly Paradises dwell;
> If ye be found obedient, and retain
> Unalterably firm his love entire
> Whose progenie you are.

Nor is Michael ignorant of God's plans for mankind, had Adam not fallen. Speaking of the possible fate of Paradise, in that better event, he says (xi, 342–6):

> This had been
> Perhaps thy Capital Seate, from whence had spred
> All generations, and had hither come
> From all the ends of th'Earth, to celebrate
> And reverence thee thir great Progenitor.

Milton would have us understand therefore that the life of Adam and Eve in Paradise was anything but final. It was a temporary affair and would have begun to change and to grow richer if they had resisted the attack of Satan. Once recognized as temporary, it is far less an object of ridicule.

It may be retorted that the passages in question occur too late, and only after our conceptions of life in Paradise have been fixed in Books Three and Four. Even so, those who have ridiculed that life have missed an essential quality of it, namely that it does not claim to be ordinary life, being simply and essentially a honeymoon. Now a honeymoon is in its nature a temporary phase; and a description of it leads on quite naturally to later remarks on other and maturer human states approaching the angelic.

But it remains to show from Milton's text that he did indeed wish us to think of life in Paradise as a honeymoon.

Adam and Eve first meet us through God's eye. The Father sees (iii, 65–9)

> Our two first Parents, yet the onely two
> Of mankind, in the happie Garden plac't,
> Reaping immortal fruits of joy and love,
> Uninterrupted joy, unrivald love
> In blissful solitude.

Unrivald love in blissful solitude. Their love was (at any rate for the moment) self-sufficient. Nothing is said of any work they should do, though it is implied that the stage of being the only two of mankind will not last. When Adam and Eve are described directly (iv, 288–355), they confirm God's vision. They are in the earliest stage of married bliss:

> Nor gentle purpose, nor endearing smiles
> Wanted, nor youthful dalliance as beseems
> Fair couple, linkt in happie nuptial League,
> Alone as they.

Their gardening is not yet serious work but is mere recreation to set off their love-making:

> By a fresh Fountain side
> They sat them down, and after no more toil
> Of their sweet Gardning labour than suffic'd
> To recommend coole Zephyr, and made ease
> More easie, wholesom thirst and appetite
> More grateful, to thir Supper Fruits they fell.

In the light of this passage, it is inept to accuse Adam and Eve's job in Paradise of being dull. They were on holiday, and they had no job. It is true that later in the book (618–33) Adam speaks of man being distinguished from beast through having appointed tasks. And he is serious enough when he speaks of early rising in order to tend the trees. But he also knows that any care they give is a mere token assertion of man's dignity, not anything practical, for two pairs of hands can make no substantial impression on the area of Paradise. There is no real denial of the holiday state.

Now just as this gardening, pursued casually, is the token of man's principal labour to come, so too the courtship is the token of future generation. Eve, after her first speech in the whole poem, is called 'our general Mother'. And Raphael's first address to her (v, 388–91) is

> Haile Mother of Mankind, whose fruitful Womb
> Shall fill the World more numerous with thy Sons
> Then with these various fruits the Trees of God
> Have heap'd this Table.

Eve's life in Paradise is a holiday before the serious business of generation. Nor is it for nothing that Raphael associated Eve's fertility with that of the earth. Paradise is not only the Garden of *Genesis*; it is also Spenser's Garden of Adonis, the seminary of all creation. And to such a seminary it is ridiculous to apply the standards of developed life in the world we know. Those standards have their turn later in the poem. Judged by the embryonic standards of the honeymoon, life in Paradise is entirely appropriate.

In speaking of these embryonic standards I am not denying my contention in my section on the *Crisis of Paradise Lost* that Adam and Eve are virtually fallen before ever they eat the apple. The fallen state can enter the limited, temporary, embryonic world of the honeymoon just as easily as the world of wider experience. Eve allowing Adam to kiss away the tears her evil dream has provoked is not any less a honeymoon figure because they betrayed that the dream had found some, however small, response in her heart.

'Or o're the tiles'

a Note on Milton's Humour

Extreme pleasant in his conversation, and at dinner, supper, etc.: but Satyricall (John Aubrey, *Minutes of the Life of Mr John Milton*)

IN my sections on the *Crisis of Paradise Lost* and the *Private Correspondence and Academic Exercises* I write incidentally on Milton's humour. This note is intended to supplement or correct those incidental remarks.

It has been a common habit to deny to Milton a sense of humour; and for two principal reasons. First Puritanism and humour were often thought incompatible; and secondly Milton's humour was confused with his wit.

It will probably now be granted that some Roundheads could possess humour just as some Cavaliers could lack it. So there is no need to comment on the first reason. With the second it is otherwise.

Now it must be conceded that in a few places Milton exploited a kind of wit, consisting largely of puns, for which we have now very little use. The longest specimens are the second poem on the death of Hobson and the scoffing speeches of Satan and Belial about their newly-invented artillery in the sixth book of *Paradise Lost*. The root idea of the Hobson poems is that while Hobson was on the move between Cambridge and London, Death could not get him: only when he rested had Death a chance. Milton plays variations on this theme with great verbal ingenuity, of which the following is a sufficient sample:

> Rest that gives all men life, gave him his death,
> And too much breathing put him out of breath;
> Nor were it contradiction to affirm
> Too long vacation hastned on his term.

And when the devils' artillery knocks the angels over, Belial ('in gamesom mood') exclaims:

Leader, the terms we sent were terms of weight,
Of hard contents, and full of force urg'd home,
Such as we might perceive amus'd them all
And stumbl'd many; who receives them right
Had need from head to foot will understand;
Not understood, this gift they have besides,
They show us when our foes walk not upright.

When the reader remembers that *amused* could also mean *bemused*, and *understand* could also mean *support* (in the physical sense), he can see that the whole passage has two separate meanings, that it is a sustained pun. We have therefore to do, not with any kind of humour but with a set exercise of verbal ingenuity, and to say that a man who practised it could not have a sense of humour is to make connections where none exists. It is moreover to apply to Milton standards from which Shakespeare is exempt. In *Twelfth Night*, answering Sir Toby's admonition to her, 'Taste your legges, sir, put them in motion,' Viola anticipates one of Belial's puns with 'My legges do better understand me, sir, than I understand what you meane by bidding me taste my legs.' And by modern liking no pun could be worse than Imogen's in a pathetic passage in *Cymbeline*, 'Why tender'st thou that Paper to me, with a look untender?' Yet Shakespeare is not on these accounts denied a sense of humour.

We have of course to do both in Shakespeare and in Milton with a habit of rhetoric, once dearly prized and widely practised, which Addison attacked in his essay on true and false wit, and for which we now have a strong distaste. And it is a habit which has no bearing either way on whether a man has a sense of humour. But in practice Milton's (to our thinking) bad puns have been allowed to have a very important bearing on the matter of his humour and have persuaded readers to think that in any passage where Milton is intentionally or unintentionally humorous he must be bad; as where the thief, robbing the rich burgher 'in at the window climbs, or o're the tiles', or the elephant to amuse Adam and Eve 'us'd all his might, and wreathed his Lithe Proboscis'. The best corrective is to look closer and with less prejudiced eyes; and I now go on to examine the whole context of the first of these two passages.

The thief robs the burgher early in Book Four (188–192); and the lines come between Satan's tortured speech on Mount Niphates and the long description of the interior of Paradise, and they form part of a necessary transition from the one to the other.[1] Satan's speech is terrific, ranging from fierce though barren remorse to a confession of bottomless misery and an outburst of hate and vengeful vows. It conveys with surpassing force the tragedy of Satan and that mania which, however tragic, is not exempt from a touch of the ridiculous; for while he spoke, his passions altered his face and betrayed to the watchful Uriel the devil beneath the disguise of the stripling cherub. Uriel noticed 'his gestures fierce and mad demeanour'. But such stormy and tragic passions are alien to Milton's (necessarily in this context) idyllic description of Paradise, and he must create a transition. And he does so by touches of humour which, initially appropriate through the ridiculous side of Satan, end by leading us gently away from that tragic and stormy side of him which could only ruin a description of unfallen Paradise. First, Satan scans the outside of Paradise,

> whose hairie sides
> With thicket overgrown, grottesque and wilde,
> Access deni'd.

And in such a context there is no harm in remembering Satan's furious words. But then the description begins to soften, and we hear of the sweet smells that drift over from within Paradise. Milton widens the context when he compares Satan savouring these smells to mariners meeting the spicy winds blowing off Arabia Felix. And then he adds his first touch of the comic:

> So entertaind those odorous sweets the Fiend
> Who came their bane, though with them better pleas'd

---

[1] Shakespeare had the same problem of a transition in the *Winter's Tale*. He had to pass from tragic Sicily to the idyllic Bohemian coast. His method is just that of Milton in this place. See my *Shakespeare's Last Plays* (London, 1938), 77–8.

> Then *Asmodeus* with the fishie fume,
> That drove him, though enamourd, from the Spouse
> Of *Tobit's* son, and with a vengeance sent
> From *Media* post to *Aegypt*, there fast bound.

It is perfectly natural (man being prone to compare and to contrast simultaneously) that one fiend, attracted by the noble and delicious odours of Paradise, should be approximated to another fiend put to flight by a low (were there fried fish shops in Milton's England?) and nauseating stench. We may doubtless infer that Asmodeus was greatly incensed at his undignified defeat; with the result that Satan's anger too has lost most of its dignity. And this is precisely what Milton intended. Coming to the foot of the actual mount of Paradise, Satan finds his way quite barred by the tangle of undergrowth and that the only gate is on the other side. Forgetful of dignity, which would demand entrance by the gate,

> Due entrance he disdaind, and in contempt,
> At one slight bound high overleap'd all bound
> Of Hill or highest Wall.

The pun on *bound* deliberately serves to lower the tension of the passage. And Milton can now lower Satan still a little more by comparing him first to a hungry wolf leaping over the hurdles of a sheep-cote, and then to a thief breaking into the house of a wealthy burgher; the comparison up to which these remarks have been leading:

> Or as a Thief bent to unhoord the cash
> Of some rich Burgher, whose substantial dores,
> Cross-barrd and bolted fast, fear no assault,
> In at the window climbes, or o're the tiles.

It is not merely that Milton wants to lower Satan's dignity once more by comparing him to a contemporary London burglar; he places him in a frankly comic setting. The rich Burgher is a comic, mildly satirized figure, whose imagination forestalled direct assault but did not extend to the ingenuity of a cat-burglar. The passage thus understood, *or o're the tiles* is a perfect touch of deliberate comedy. We are now

74

well prepared for Satan to assume the form of no more digni-
fied bird than a cormorant and to leave him perched on the
highest tree of the garden. Comedy has diverted our minds
from the tragic and the heroic, and we are in a frame of mind
not hostile to hearing the great description of Paradise that
follows.

It turns out therefore that a passage often condemned as
unintentionally ridiculous contains in itself a pleasant piece of
humour and in so doing co-operates with other passages in
manipulating a necessary major transition.

Actually, we have met Milton's burgher before in perhaps
the most charming and genially satirical piece of his prose: the
rich Protestant merchant in *Areopagitica*, who 'addicted to his
pleasure and to his profits, finds Religion to be a traffick so
entangl'd, and of so many piddling accounts, that of all
mysteries he cannot skill to keep a stock going upon that
trade'. So he hires a Divine to do the job for him:

> To him he adheres, resigns the whole warehouse of his religion,
> with all the locks and keyes into his custody. . . . He entertains
> him; gives him gifts, feasts him, lodges him; his religion comes
> home at night, praies, is liberally supt, and sumptuously laid to
> sleep, rises, is saluted, and after the malmsey, or some well spic't
> bruage, and better breakfasted then he whose appetite would
> have gladly fed on green figs between *Bethany* and *Jerusalem*, his
> Religion walks abroad at eight, and leaves his kind entertainer
> in the shop trading all day without his religion.[1]

This burgher, thinking himself secure on the religious side by
his simple-minded precautions and yet being so vulnerable, is
very like the other burgher who is robbed against his expectations.

I do not see how any honest reader could deny Milton a
sense of humour in the two passages I have been discussing;
but this does not mean that Milton habitually wrote thus.
When it comes to a general verdict, I should say that Milton
shows more humour than is supposed and that this humour is
usually of a certain kind.

[1] iv, 333–4.

In the richest comedy the various discrepancies—between appearance and reality, pretensions and actions, imagined and true motives, and so on—that provoke us to laugh or titter or smile are shown through most of the characters. In the *Miller's Tale* the Carpenter is one of several comic victims; in *Emma* the heroine, for all her charm, is no more exempt from the comic pitfall than Miss Bates. Such richness we cannot look for in Milton; and since the comic victimization is less broken up and parcelled out it produces a grimmer and more satirical effect. Sometimes indeed it will be a question whether the effect is humorous or not. I will give an instance which I find humorous myself but which others might well not think so.

The eleventh book of *Paradise Lost* concerns Adam's education, through a series of visions, to fit him for life's trials in a world now very different from Paradise. These visions are a series of 'examples' in the medieval and Elizabethan sense, pointing morals of what to seek and what to shun. But to Adam's untrained eye they do not convey the right lesson at once. Adam is the victim of appearance as against reality and needs angelic instruction. The visions are mostly grim enough, but there is something comic in the ingenuous way Adam takes them. First, he sees Cain murder Abel; and he exclaims in horror, 'Is Pietie thus and pure Devotion paid?', and Michael has to reassure him that the final reckoning will be far other. Then he sees the lazar-house and men dying of painful diseases; and Michael has to comfort him with the thought that death need not come so terribly as that. Then comes a gay scene of love and marriage with feast and music, and Adam once again falls into the snare of confusing appearance and reality:

> Such happy interview and fair event
> Of love and youth not lost, Songs, Garlands, Flours,
> And charming Symphonies attach'd the heart
> Of *Adam*, soon enclin'd to admit delight,
> The bent of Nature; which he thus express'd.
> True opener of mine eyes, prime Angel blest,
> Much better seems this vision.

True opener of mine eyes is cruelly and beautifully ironical at

Adam's expense. He thinks Michael has presented to his senses a true vision of happy peaceful life, when actually Michael will open his eyes wider and most unpleasantly by explaining that these lovely women are bad within ('fair atheists') and that their sins will find them out.

Some readers may think that Milton is too cruel to Adam for the episode to have humour. But Adam had brought trouble on himself, and Milton does somehow fulfil that requirement of all true humour: a potential identification of the writer's self with the comic victim. For the true humorist must be the very opposite of Lucretius's philosophical man watching from the safety of the shore the struggles of the man in the sea below him. The humorist does indeed watch the man's plight but with the added thought that it is the common lot and that it may be his turn next. Let me illustrate Milton's position from another place in *Paradise Lost*. Those who think his Paradise of Fools in Book Three nothing more than an astonishing but misguided piece of virtuosity, animated by a hatred of Catholicism, forget that he characterized the place as 'to few unknown long after'. In other words we all, or nearly all, Milton included, inhabit that region at one time or another. 'The Eremits and Friers White, Black, and Grey, with all their trumperie' are but emblems of a universal folly. So, too, was Adam's pathetic confusion of appearance and reality a universal human failing. Milton may laugh at it but he cannot do so cruelly, for he includes himself in the object of mirth.

This capacity to see himself as the comic victim comes out in his letter to Peter Heimbach written in the Plague Year.[1] Heimbach had heard a rumour that Milton had died of the plague and had written for news. Milton speaks of himself as follows:

> I am delighted to find that you have remembered me after so long a time, although, to judge by your elaborate compliments, there seems some reason to suspect that you do not remember me very clearly, since you express your admiration for the union in

[1] Milton, *Private Correspondence and Academic Exercises*, translated by P. B. Tillyard (Cambridge, 1932), 51.

my person of so many virtues which are incompatible. For my part, I should dread too large a family as the result of so many unions, if it were not common knowledge that virtues grow and flourish best in poverty and hardships. One of those virtues, however, has not requited me very handsomely for my hospitality. For the virtue you call statesmanship (but which I would rather have you call loyalty to my country), after captivating me with her fair-sounding name, has, so to speak, almost left me without a country. However, the chorus of the others makes a fine harmony. One's country is wherever it is well with one.

Here Milton treats himself much as Michael treats Adam. He scores off his old self that used to picture fine results from the efforts of the active and contemplative virtues it commanded. Now they merely make up a fine chorus in the complimentary and extravagant letter of a friend. Love of his country presented a fine but specious appearance; the reality is quite different to him now, for his whole idea of what his country is has changed. The gap between his ideals and his achievement has an element of the ridiculous. If Milton can be so hard on himself in this letter, he is not being too hard on Adam in the eleventh book of *Paradise Lost*. Some sort of humour should be allowed to both passages in question. And it is this sort that peculiarly belongs to Milton.

Finally, Milton practised with high skill a kind of grotesque juxtaposition, belonging to the borderland of wit and humour. I can introduce the topic through a passage which has called forth some detailed comment. It is part of the account in Book Ten of *Paradise Lost* of Sin and Death building their causeway from Hell to the universe:

> The aggregated Soyle
> Death with his Mace petrific, cold and dry,
> As with a Trident smote, and fix't as firm
> As *Delos* floating once; the rest his look
> Bound with *Gorgonian* rigor not to move,
> And with *Asphaltic* slime; broad as the Gate,
> Deep to the Roots of Hell the gather'd beach
> They fasten'd.[1]

[1] 293–300.

78

It is the middle sentence in this passage ('the rest' . . .
'*Asphaltic slime*') with which I am concerned, and which has
troubled some commentators.

First, Bentley could not put up with the notion of a look
binding with asphaltic slime. Certainly a look is a flimsy
agent of so material an operation. Pearce, against his usual
practice, yielded to Bentley and by repunctuation connected
'*Asphaltic* slime' with what follows. Such a change, causing a
pause in the reading after 'move' and a run-on from '*Asphaltic*
slime' to 'broad as the Gate, etc.' is so disastrous and un-
Miltonic rhythmically that it cannot be thought of. It is much
better to read more laxly and not to connect Death's look
too closely with the slime, taking it that Death, in a way not
specified, worked in the bitumen. William Empson[1] has included this passage in a more general attack on Milton's con-
founding of abstract and concrete, of antique ingenuousness
and Augustan complacency in scientific superiority. The yoking of '*Gorgonian* rigor' and '*Asphaltic slime*' is indeed sympto-
matic of some wide habit of mind, but I doubt if Empson has
described it aright. Surely what he attacks is the element of
baroque exaggeration which has been too little recognized in
Milton. Empson, with his admirably catholic taste, cannot
fail to appreciate the baroque, but surely he errs in thinking
Milton too little conscious of his confusions to qualify for the
evident sophistication of the baroque artist. I should say myself that ever since his first *Prolusion* Milton showed a taste
for the slightly grotesque juxtaposition and was fully conscious of it. For instance, parallel to the yoking of abstract
and concrete in the passage under review is the mixture of
scientific latinization and homespun directness in these lines:

> The Sun that light imparts to all, receives
> From all his alimental recompense
> In humid exhalations, and at Even
> Sups with the Ocean. (P.L., v, 423–6.)

The scientific and astronomical sun almost turns into a
Puritan merchant relaxing after a long day's work in the

[1] *Some Versions of Pastoral* (London, 1935), 154.

counting house. And Milton *intended* a touch of the grotesque. It was with just the same intention that he added the bathos of concreteness to the nobility of the 'Gorgonian rigor'.

There is another passage where Milton uses the sun for a quaint and semi-humorous contrast. It is in Book Seven of *Paradise Lost* and it describes the sun's creation and power and the subservience of the lesser lights to it:

> Of Light by farr the greater part he took,
> Transplanted from her cloudie Shrine, and plac'd
> In the Suns Orb, made porous to receive
> And drink the liquid Light, firm to retaine
> Her gather'd beams, great Palace now of Light.
> Hither as to thir Fountain other Starrs
> Repairing, in thir gold'n Urns draw Light,
> And hence the Morning Planet guilds his horns;
> By tincture or reflection they augment
> Thir small peculiar, though from human sight
> So farr remote, with diminution seen.
> First in his East the glorious Lamp was seen,
> Regent of Day. (359–71.)

Here the little officious stars are fussily latinized ('by tincture or reflection they augment their small peculiar') and hence contrasted with the forthright majesty of the sun.

And here Milton does the same kind of thing but on a larger scale. When Michael showed Adam the Flood he told him what would be the fate of the mount of Paradise, on which they are standing:

> Then shall this Mount
> Of Paradise by might of Waves be moovd
> Out of his place, pushd by the horned flood,
> With all his verdure spoil'd, and Trees adrift
> Down the great River to the op'ning Gulf,
> And there take root an Iland salt and bare,
> The haunt of Seales and Orcs, and Sea-mews clang.
> To teach thee that God attributes to place
> No sanctitie, if none be thither brought
> By Men who there frequent, or therein dwell.
> And now what further shall ensue, behold.

> He lookd, and saw the Ark hull on the flood,
> Which now abated, for the Clouds were fled,
> Drivn by a keen North-winde, that blowing drie
> Wrinkl'd the face of Deluge, as decai'd. (xi, 829–43)

To sandwich a highly didactic piece of Protestantism between two highly romantic pieces of description was to administer a severe shock to the reader. Commenting on the passage else-where[1] I said that if such juxtapositions were very frequent Milton would be a kind of colossal, unconscious humorist. I now think that they are fairly frequent in *Paradise Lost* and that in staging them Milton was fully conscious of his act, and that the act itself contains an element of humour.

[1] *The Miltonic Setting* (Cambridge, 1938), 57–8.

The Action of Comus

1. Introductory

THE centre of *Comus* is the scene where the Lady, imprisoned in the magic chair, conducts an argument with the Enchanter on the subject of chastity. It is disputed who had the best of it. Professedly the Lady, and Comus is made to admit it; but Comus speaks so well that Milton has been accused of being here (as elsewhere) on the Devil's side without knowing it. Beneath every opinion is the assumption that one or other of the disputants is right; Milton being singled out from the great poets as the one to whom the privilege of being on both or on neither side at the same time must be denied. The assumption is false. Comus and the Lady are both wrong, or, if right, in ways they did not perceive. And if Milton is on the Devil's side at any point, he knew very well what he was doing. Not till the final words of the Attendant Spirit is the truth revealed.

If these contentions could be proved they change the action of the masque. *Comus*, instead of being an academic dispute ending in stalemate or at best in an unexciting victory with a final dose of lyricism to anaesthetize the reader's critical fastidiousness, will have a plot that answers all the previous questions. What follows is my case for this hypothesis.

2. The Texts of 1634 and 1637

The crucial passage is the Attendant Spirit's epilogue (line 976 'To the ocean now I fly' to the end); and unfortunately this is one of the few places in the whole poem where there are serious textual variations. These must first be pointed out.

Comus was performed at Michaelmas 1634, but it was not printed till 1637. The earliest printed edition agrees substantially with the later editions and thus represents Milton's final recension.[1] There are two manuscript versions, one preserved, with other writings of Milton, in the Trinity Manuscript, the other once in the possession of the family in whose honour *Comus* was written and known as the Bridgewater or Egerton Manuscript. The latter, containing a slightly altered and abbreviated version for stage production, need not concern us. The various changes within the Trinity Manuscript have no decisive importance; and the significant changes are those between the completed first draft as contained in the Trinity Manuscript (which I call the first or 1634 version) and the first printed text (which I call the 1637 version). These changes consist of additions to the Lady's refutation of Comus and to the Spirit's epilogue; and it is just in these added lines that I find the clue to the way Milton meant us to interpret the debate between Comus and the Lady. I must therefore go on to discuss them.

In the Trinity Manuscript the Lady begins her last speech to Comus in answer to his grand tirade on the bounties of nature and the unnaturalness of virginity, in the words we know, 'I had not thought to have unlockt my lips in this unhallow'd air', and goes on to defend temperance against luxury. But when she reaches her climax on this theme,

> for swinish gluttony
> Ne're looks to Heav'n amidst his gorgeous feast,
> But with besotted base ingratitude
> Cramms, and blasphemes his feeder,

she ends and Comus replies, as at the end of line 806 in the version we know,

> Com, no more,
> This is meer moral babble, and direct
> Against the canon laws of our foundation.

The Lady's defence of the sun-clad power of chastity and of the sage and serious doctrine of virginity, with Comus's ad-

[1] For convenient summaries of the textual variants of *Comus*, referring to previous discussions, see John S. Diekhoff in *Publications of the Modern Language Association of America*, 1937, pp. 705, 725ff. My remarks here on the texts are abbreviated from my original version in *Essays and Studies*.

mission (spoken aside) that she fables not and that he is frightened, are not there, being added in the 1637 edition. The epilogue begins in the Trinity Manuscript in the familiar way, 'To the ocean now I fly', and goes on to talk of the Hesperian gardens. Four lines (984–7) from the description of them are not in the manuscript but were added in 1637. These are ornamental, not important for the general meaning. But a little after, in describing Iris, the manuscript begins to differ from the familiar version, reading as follows:

> Iris there with humid bow
> Waters the odorous banks that blow
> Flowers of more mingled hew
> Than her purfl'd scarfe can shew,
> Yellow, watchet, greene, and blew,
> And drenches oft with manna dew
> Beds of Hyacinth, and roses,
> Where many a cherub soft reposes.

And omitting all reference to the Garden of Adonis, Venus, Cupid and Psyche, the manuscript goes on to the last lines of all, 'Now my message well is done'. The 1637 edition added the lines on the Garden of Adonis, and in the passage just quoted altered *many a cherub* to *young Adonis*; and for *Yellow, watchet, greene, and blew* substituted *List mortals, if your ears be true*, to draw attention to the special allegorical significance of the Adonis passage.

3. *The Reason for the* 1637 *Additions*

Why did Milton add these two passages between 1634 and 1637? If the first passage stood alone, we might answer very simply: to give sufficient weight to the Lady's reply to Comus. In the early version she had answered only his arguments for profusion and luxury, not his cheapening of 'that same vaunted name Virginity', and something on the latter subject too would give better balance. But the second addition admits of no such explanation. First, the deliberate exhortation 'List mortals, if your ears be true' shows that Milton thought the meaning important and wanted it heeded. And secondly, the passage itself points to high and solemn themes. It was Thomas Warton who noticed that the passage referred to Spenser's account of the Garden of Adonis in the sixth canto of the third book of the *Faerie Queene*, and his contention has not been disputed; but I doubt if people have realized how much this reference amounts to. But first for the truth of the reference: we must have no doubts of that if we are to give much weight to the passage. Iris, wrote Milton, in the paradisiac region where the Attendant Spirit will return,

> drenches with *Elysian* dew
> (List mortals, if your ears be true)
> Beds of *Hyacinth*, and roses
> Where young *Adonis* oft reposes
> Waxing well of his deep wound
> In slumber soft, and on the ground
> Sadly sits th' *Assyrian* Queen:
> But far above in spangled sheen
> Celestial *Cupid* her fam'd son advanc't,
> Holds his dear *Psyche* sweet intranc't,
> After her wandring labours long,
> Till free consent the gods among
> Make her his eternal Bride,
> And from her fair unspotted side
> Two blissful twins are to be born,
> Youth and Joy; so *Jove* hath sworn.

Spenser's Garden of Adonis consists of an outer realm, the seminary of all created things, and of an inner sanctuary, over-grown with hyacinth and other plants, where Venus, mistress of the garden, enjoys the love of Adonis, the boar which wounded him now being bound in a 'strong rocky cave' hewn beneath the mountain on which the bower is situated. It is to this inner sanctuary, described in stanzas 45 to 50, that Milton refers, but he varies his version by imagining an earlier moment before Adonis is quite healed of his wound. Cupid, too, inhabits Spenser's Garden of Adonis with his Psyche, who has already borne him a child, Pleasure. Milton again varies by putting the marriage in the future and foretelling a second child, Youth, as the offspring of it. The component parts of the two passages are mythological commonplaces, accessible to any poet, but the identity of the parts themselves, the above variations excepted, and the order they are arranged in are so close that I can see no alternative to Milton's intending a reference to Spenser.

To perceive what such a reference meant, we must consider Milton's readers. In the year 1637 Spenser was still the great modern poet. It was no longer the fashion to imitate his style, but he was the unchallenged poetic classic of modern English literature, and everyone read him. Now the episode of the births of Belphoebe and Amoret and of the Garden of Adonis was one of the most famous in the whole of the *Faerie Queene*. When Milton wrote *Comus* the *Faerie Queene* had been published upward of forty years, and its familiarity would be roughly that of one of the best-known episodes from the *Pickwick Papers*, say the case of Bardell *v.* Pickwick, in the year 1880; while the more restricted passage to which Milton refers would be as familiar as Sam Weller's evidence in that same trial. Further we must remember that Milton's readers were nearer to the Middle Ages than to ourselves in their readiness to allegorize classical myth. For all his modernity Bacon could write the *Wisdom of the Ancients*, which to a modern is a tissue of dreary and unprofitable fantasy. Here is a typical passage:

> Pan's crook also contains a fine representation of the ways of nature, which are partly straight and partly crooked; thus the staff, having an extraordinary bend towards the top, denotes that the works of divine providence are generally brought about by remote means or in a circuit, as if somewhat else were intended than the effect produced, as in the sending of Joseph into Egypt etc. So likewise in human government they who sit at the helm manage and wind the people more successfully by pretext and oblique courses than by such as are direct and straight; so that in effect all sceptres are crooked at the top.

Bacon did not mean this to be funny, nor would Milton's contemporaries have taken him otherwise than seriously. Bred to such ways of thinking about allegory, contemporary readers of *Comus* would have been eager to get the hidden meaning of the passage to which the Attendant Spirit calls special notice.

For the above reasons Milton's second important addition to *Comus* would have stood out as a most significant passage, the very reverse of lyrical sedative and able to give a decisive turn to the meaning of the whole poem.

4. *The First Version of Comus*

Up to the time of *Comus*, Milton's longest poetical exercise had been *L'Allegro* and *Il Penseroso*. These, I have argued, are modelled on the form of the university prolusion or disputation, *L'Allegro* being in praise of day and *Il Penseroso* of night. There is no third section attempting to reconcile the two pleas. It was quite natural that Milton should use the same technique for constructing the first version of *Comus*. There are of course complications, but the centre of the masque is an academic disputation for and against chastity, with the Lady and Comus as disputants. Milton was doing nothing new in treating the topic in this argumentative way; Marlowe, for instance, is much more academic when he makes Leander argue thus with Hero:

> This idol which you term virginity
> Is neither essence subject to the eye,
> No, nor to any one exterior sense,
> Nor hath it any place of residence,
> Nor is't of earth or mould celestial,
> Or capable of any form at all.
> Of that which hath no being, do not boast:
> Things that are not at all, are never lost.

Now the disputant might be called on to support either side of a debated question: he was not expected to say what he happened to think himself. Thus Milton is impartial in his treatment of day and night in *L'Allegro* and *Il Penseroso*. It may be that this habit of impartiality helped him to make his Comus put his case so well. Milton of course takes sides, and the Lady is made to win. But her victory is not at all emphatic; half Comus's plea is unanswered. And the rest of the masque does nothing to answer his declaration that beauty such as the

Lady's could be better employed than in spinning or embroidery. It is in structure no more than the coda to a piece of action already concluded.

But though structurally the 1634 *Comus* was an elaborated university disputation, it is in some ways more serious than *L'Allegro* and *Il Penseroso*. Milton has emerged from the relatively personal and local to the public and the traditional. The allegorizing of Circe's herd into human beings subdued by one or other form of sensuality must have begun in Greek times. It was a commonplace of the Christian classicizers; it was a medieval possession through Boethius; and it was popular in the Renaissance. Milton in using a variant of the theme competes with all western literature, just as in choosing the masque form he adopted a standard that had been exalted by the genius of Ben Jonson. He is using public material too in expressing the perplexities and perils of life through the allegory of a dark and tangled forest. In particular he is beginning to compete with Spenser.

Even more important, Milton in *Comus* resembles the greatest Elizabethans in giving us man in his cosmic setting, in his middle position on the great chain of being between the beasts and the angels and attuned in his own microcosm to all the great happenings of the enveloping universe. It is somewhat ironic that of all the characters Comus should do most to help this process. But we must remember that Comus was a god, that the classical gods were orthodox devils in disguise, and that the Devil himself is the chief ape of the Almighty. Comus indeed succeeds wonderfully in expressing the great cosmic commonplaces worthily while giving himself away as an impostor.

> We that are of purer fire
> Imitate the Starry Quire,
> Who in their nightly watchfull Sphears,
> Lead in swift round the Months and Years.
> The Sounds, and Seas with all their finny drove
> Now to the Moon in wavering Morrice move,
> And on the Tawny Sands and Shelves,
> Trip the pert Fairies and the dapper Elves;

> By dimpled Brook, and Fountain brim,
> The Wood-Nymphs deckt with Daisies trim,
> Their merry wakes and pastimes keep.

Comus here speaks of the traditional picture of the whole universe as one great dance, from the highest angel dancing round God's throne to the humble vine wreathing the elm in its own rhythm or the wind blowing the dust in eddies: the picture given with such compelling charm by Sir John Davies in his *Orchestra* or hinted at in Daedalus's first song in Jonson's masque of *Pleasure Reconciled to Virtue*. But what impudence in Comus to claim that his own disorderly revels are tuned to the music of the spheres and keep the measure of the planets and the tides! The imposture is patent. Again, when Comus makes his great speech to the Lady (line 706, 'O foolishnes of men') and praises the bounty of nature, he is in the tradition of the Fathers of the Church praising the wonders of God's creation in their commentaries on *Genesis* or of the medieval theologians advising their disciples to repair the error of their first parents by seeking God in his works, *per speculum creaturarum*. He is also competing with Spenser who, himself in this same tradition, described the plenitude of God's creation in the canto of the *Faerie Queene* already referred to, with a rapture equalled only by Milton himself when he came to describe the 'enormous bliss' of Eden in *Paradise Lost*. But here again Comus overdoes it, ending his description with a riot of hyperboles that suggest he has been drinking:

> Th'earth cumber'd and the wing'd air dark't with plumes;
> The herds would over-multitude their Lords,
> The Sea o'refraught would swell, and th'unsought diamonds
> Would so emblaze the forhead of the Deep,
> And so bestudd with Stars, that they below
> Would grow inur'd to light, and com at last
> To gaze upon the Sun with shameless brows.

Comus then is more serious in substance than *L'Allegro* and *Il Penseroso* and as such demanded a more emphatic conclusion than the 1634 version provided.

5. *The Final Version of Comus*

The changes Milton made in the 1637 version mainly concern the central theme of chastity. And I must comment on the doctrine of chastity as he conceived it. We must remember that chastity had a wider meaning in Milton's day than in ours. It meant monogamy as well as virginity. The matter is made particularly clear in a poem well known to Milton, Phineas Fletcher's *Purple Island*.[1] Among the various mental qualities personified and described allegorically in this poem are twin ladies: Agnia and Parthenia.[2] Agnia, who is Chastity in the married, is mild and modest, and she wears no armour.

> Upon her arched brow unarmed Love
> Triumphing sat in peaceful victory.

Her emblem is a pair of turtle doves. She receives four stanzas of description. Parthenia, who gets much more attention, is Virginity, or Chastity in the single; and she is militant.

> With her, her sister went, a warlike maid,
> Parthenia, all in steel and gilded arms;
> In needle's stead a might spear she sway'd,
> With which in bloody fields and fierce alarms
> The boldest champion she down would bear,
> And like a thunderbolt wide passage tear,
> Flinging all to the earth with her enchanted spear.

She is dazzlingly fair, hotly pursued, but chooses a heavenly not an earthly lover.

> A thousand knights woo'd her with busy pain,
> To thousand she her virgin grant deni'd,
> Although her dear-sought love to entertain
> They all their wit and all their strength appli'd:
> Yet in her heart love close his sceptre sway'd,
> That to an heavenly spouse her thoughts betray'd,
> Where she a maiden wife might live and wifely maid.

[1] Published in 1633 but written earlier. Giles and Phineas Fletcher were closely connected with Cambridge. Milton would certainly have read the *Purple Island* in manuscript years before he wrote *Comus*.

[2] Canto X, stanzas 24–40.

It is Parthenia that Milton celebrates in his first version of *Comus* through the Elder Brother's speech. Chastity there is like the huntress Diana, like Minerva with her Gorgon-shield, both militant goddesses, and in the end she gives her votaries peculiar powers.

In the revised poem the lines added to the Lady's speech are a fierce defence of chastity. And beyond doubt she is Parthenia. It is the sage and serious doctrine of *virginity* that she defends. And she is extremely fierce, speaking of her rapt spirits being kindled to a flame of sacred vehemence. She is indeed Diana or Minerva in action. Chastity too is a mystery, able to give her votaries supernatural powers. It is all the more surprising therefore that the addition to the epilogue, concerning the Garden of Adonis, should be, as it is, opposed to the strict doctrine of virginity.

In expounding its sense I shall have to consider the whole Epilogue; for the added lines put a different interpretation on the existing ones they followed. The Attendant Spirit begins by saying that he will return to a realm where among other denizens are Hesperus and his three daughters; and by so doing he invites his contemporary audience to exercise their allegorical tact, for the Gardens of Hesperus were rich in mythological allegory. Research could probably unearth a wide variety of meaning put on the Gardens of Hesperus with their golden-fruited tree, which a dragon guarded and round which Hesperus's three daughters sang their songs. But there were two prevailing meanings: the paradisiac and the erotic. It was thought that the myth was a pagan reminiscence of the Garden of Eden. In Raleigh's words:

> So also was the fiction of those golden apples kept by the dragon taken from the serpent which tempted Eva. So was Paradise itself transported out of Asia into Africa and the Garden of the Hesperides.[1]

Alternatively the golden apples were symbols of fertility and love. Milton shows a knowledge of both interpretations in *Comus*. In the lines excised from the Trinity Manuscript after

[1] *History of the World*, i, 6, 4.

the fourth line of the poem the Hesperian Gardens are purely paradisiac. Here is the passage in its setting:

> Before the starrie threshold of Joves Court
> My mansion is, where those immortal shapes
> Of bright aereall spirits live insphear'd
> In regions mild of calme and serene aire,
> Amidst th'Hesperian gardens, on whose bancks
> Bedew'd with nectar and celestiall songs,
> Aeternall roses grow, and hyacinth,
> And fruits of golden rind, on whose faire tree
> The scalie-harnest dragon ever keeps
> His uninchanted eye.

But in the Second Brother's speech (lines 393–7) the erotic symbolism is obvious:

> But beauty like the fair Hesperian Tree
> Laden with blooming gold, had need the guard
> Of dragon watch with uninchanted eye,
> To save her blossoms, and defend her fruit
> From the rash hand of bold Incontinence.

When, therefore, Milton's readers met the Hesperian Gardens in the epilogue of *Comus* they would be on the alert for allegory and, though ready for pretty well anything, would be especially ready for a paradisiac or an erotic significance or for both at once. Now in the earlier version they would have found only the paradisiac significance to the point: their expectation of the other would just be allowed to drop. But not so in the revised version: there the plain fertility symbolism of the Garden of Adonis would realize the expectation of an erotic significance in the other mythical garden. In fact the whole of the revised epilogue would be concerned with love, as well as with some form of Paradise.

We are at last in a position to examine the meaning which Milton, through Spenser, put on the Garden of Adonis.

The Spenserian episode of the Garden of Adonis occurs in that great unit of the *Faerie Queene*, the third and fourth books, that deals with every form of love from bestiality to the most refined spiritual affection. Its immediate context is the story of

Belphoebe and Amoret. These two were twins, daughters of Crysogone, who conceived them miraculously from sunbeams and bore them miraculously in a sleep without pain. Girls from the train of Venus found them while their mother still slept and took them away. Diana adopted Belphoebe and brought her up in perfect maidenhead till she developed into a bright fierce virgin (the plain prototype of Phineas Fletcher's Parthenia). Venus adopted Amoret and brought her up in the inner sanctuary of the Garden of Adonis.

> Hither great Venus brought this infant fair,
> The younger daughter of Crysogone,
> And unto Psyche with great trust and care
> Committed her, yfostered to be
> And trained up in true feminity;
> Who no less carefully her tendered
> Than her own daughter Pleasure, to whom she
> Made her companion and her lessoned
> In all the lore of love and goodly womanhead.

After this education she became the

> loadstar of all chast affection
> To all fair ladies that do live on ground.

She was in fact the pattern of perfect married affection, and appears again as Fletcher's Agnia. In the end she marries Scudamour, and, bred as she was in the very origin and seminary of all earthly life, she was plainly destined to carry out God's command of 'increase and multiply' with a thoroughness calculated to satisfy the exacting procreative standards of Elizabethan England. But that is one side of the Garden of Adonis only. It was in days of Eden that God pronounced his command and in some sort this garden is heaven too. It is Psyche herself, the immortal soul, that teaches Amoret her lore; even though that lore is in part earthly. Like the soul the Garden of Adonis is the great meeting-place of the temporal and the eternal, of the shifting phenomena of nature and the eternal law under which these phenomena operate.

6. *The Meaning of the Additions*

What then did Milton mean by referring to this familiar but complicated tissue of erotic lore? May he not have meant to give the whole poem a new turn and in particular to settle the debate between Comus and the Lady?

Comus had spoken magnificently but perversely of the bounty of God. The Lady in reply had countered the perversity by a plea of moderation and of equal distribution, yet in so doing had shown less sense of that bounty than her adversary. The Attendant Spirit by mentioning the Garden of Adonis, the very workshop of nature, gives the solution. This garden has all the bounty described by Comus and all the comeliness and order insisted on by the Lady. Both disputants are shown partly right and partly wrong.

Then for the second topic, chastity. The Lady thinks herself cast for the part of Belphoebe or Parthenia; Comus would like to turn her into a Hellenore, a wanton. That is what he means when he says to her after praising her beauty,

> There was another meaning in these gifts,

and that is what she understands him to mean, and what Milton in his first version meant him to mean and her to understand him to mean. But later Milton saw that both the Lady and Comus were wrong: that there *was* another meaning in these gifts, but that it was not Comus's. The meaning was marriage. The Lady was not really cast for Belphoebe but for Amoret, not for Parthenia but for Agnia. And he conveys his correction—too obliquely for some tastes—by the Attendant Spirit's references to the Garden of Adonis where Belphoebe and Parthenia were out of place.

The gain is great. The ignorance of Comus and the Lady, explained above, becomes dramatic irony, and the whole play instead of being an unresolved debate is given a shape and a solution. The play concerns chastity and the Lady is the heroine. Comus advocates incontinence, Acrasia; the Lady advocates abstinence. The Attendant Spirit gives the solution, advocating the Aristotelian middle course, which for the

Lady is the right one; and it is marriage. This perhaps is putting the matter too baldly. The Lady's resistance to Comus is not meant to be bad, as Comus's seductions are. It is good; it may even be an act of a probation: but it is not final. The setting is aristocratic; the Lady, though but young, will one day be a great lady. She must take her place in society and do what is expected of her. And by having triumphed as Belphoebe she is free to proceed to her true part of Amoret.

This interpretation is the more probable when we remember the whole aristocratic setting of the masque-form and the specimen of it to which Milton owed most, Jonson's *Pleasure Reconciled to Virtue*. This figures Hercules routing Comus 'the god of cheer or the belly' after having killed Antaeus, and crowned for his pains by Hermes. After such labours of virtue, pleasure is no longer inept, but Virtue and Pleasure may be reconciled. A troup of twelve masquers (one of them the Prince, son of Hesperus, King of the West, *alias* James I) issue from their home in Mount Atlas, where they are being educated in austere virtue by Daedalus the wise. They are permitted to dance an allegorical measure with twelve noble ladies, Virtue and Pleasure again being reconciled. But they must return to their hill of superior and difficult education. Finally Virtue is praised in words which Milton remembered when he wrote *Comus*:

> She, she it is in darkness shines,
> 'Tis she that still herself refines
> By her own light to every eye;
> More seen, more known, when Vice stands by;
> And though a stranger here on earth,
> In heaven she hath her right of birth.

Milton's possible debt to certain details of Jonson's masque is well known, but he may have got a more general aid from it. The theme itself, the clear firm outline of the structure, the sense of social responsibility, may well have stimulated him to mend the simplicity of the first prolusional draft. In a way by his alterations Milton approximates his theme to Jonson's; only the title of *Virtue Reconciled to Pleasure* would be more appropriate. In Jonson the emphasis is on the pleasure with the warning note that the conjunction, however legitimate in its proper seasons, can be but temporary. In Milton the emphasis is on the trial and the struggle, through the winning of which Virtue may legitimately be reconciled with Pleasure, the reconciliation being just hinted at the end.

Then there is Fletcher's *Faithful Shepherdess*, of which there are various echoes in *Comus* and which, republished in 1629 and acted at Court on January 6, 1934, with Inigo Jones's setting, must have been known to Milton's audience as well as to himself. This pastoral deals with virginity, wantonness, and especially marriage; for though Clorin, the maid whose virginity gives her special powers, keeps her state for good, the action ends generally with marriage. If Milton, in writing or rewriting *Comus*, had the *Faithful Shepherdess* in mind, he would be ready to include married as well as unmarried chastity in his subject and to assume a readiness for such inclusion in his readers. He could thus afford, if it suited him, to refer to the married state in an indirect, allusive manner.

7. *Epilogue*

Aubrey records that Milton was 'extreme pleasant in conversation but Satyricall.' If Milton watched the performance of his own masque (slightly garbled to suit the music and cut to suit the actors) he may have felt some ironical amusement at witnessing an ordinary little girl sustaining the tremendous part of Belphoebe. If so, he may have felt even then the possible irony in the line

There was another meaning in these gifts,

and have had suggested to him the changes he ultimately made. Moreover, the Earl and Countess of Bridgewater, for whom he wrote the masque, were themselves the parents of an immense family of four sons and eleven daughters. The Garden of Adonis was their spiritual home. Was it not the spiritual home of their daughter Alice, too, who took the part of the Lady? All this is pure romancing, but if it happened to be true, Milton was not the only ironist. For all his added hints about wedlock, fate contrived that the Lady Alice Egerton, though she married, deceased without issue.

POSTSCRIPT

When I wrote on the action of *Comus* I had not read A. S. P. Woodhouse's profound and interesting article, *The Argument of Milton's 'Comus'* (*University of Toronto Quarterly*, vol. xi, pp. 46–71). Much of this article concerns other matters than have concerned me, but Woodhouse agrees with me on the importance of the Spenser allusion in the Epilogue while differing on the use he thinks Milton made of it.

On the interpretation of Spenser's Garden of Adonis and of what both pairs in it (Venus and Adonis, Cupid and Psyche) mean we are agreed. He wrote (pp. 68–9):

> For Spenser the story of Venus and Adonis represents the spirit of love and the principle of generation operating throughout the natural order; and the story of Cupid and Psyche should somehow represent the same spirit and principle in their specifically human application, which is marriage with its productiveness and legitimate pleasure, opposed . . . to the illegitimate pleasures of Acrasia, at war with productiveness.

Woodhouse thinks that Milton accepts Spenser's presentation of the Garden of Adonis as far as nature is concerned. That garden refutes Comus's bogus plea for the virtue of nature's bounty, as it confutes Acrasia. And here again we agree. But he thinks Milton's Cupid and Psyche different from Spenser's and that unlike Spenser Milton does not refer in the Epilogue to marriage. In support he points to Milton's Cupid being *celestial*. Cupid is not the marriage-god but the Love-god of Plato. The trouble here is that his and Psyche's children are the very un-Platonic pair, Youth and Joy. For this trouble Woodhouse has an ingenious explanation. Now Milton's *Joy* is so plain an equivalent of Spenser's *Pleasure*, and Spenser's Pleasure so patently represents the marriage-bed that I find any other explanation than an erotic one very hard to accept. On the other hand it is not easy to give a predominantly human significance to Milton's *celestial* Cupid who sits far above his mother. But one *can* say that Venus and Adonis represent life below

97

the human and the reproduction of such life, while Cupid representing human love is thus above Venus and is celestial because the human soul is a piece of divinity. There are difficulties in any explanation, but the whole trend of the Spenserian original in its proper context is so eminently concerned with marriage that I find it hard to believe that Milton in recalling it could have gone so flatly against that prime concern.

With Woodhouse's contention that Milton in *Comus* was distinguishing between the realm of nature and the realm of grace I incline to agree. But I cannot agree that the last three couplets of the masque ('Mortals that would follow me', etc.) refer to the realm of grace specifically. They do not crown thought; they dismiss the audience. And the tone of such a dismissal simply dictates that the sentiment expressed should be general. The freedom that virtue brings in these lines is neither the freedom from the blows of fate achieved by the virtue of the stoic nor the specifically Christian freedom, but just freedom. Woodhouse's argument rests considerably on these last lines; deprived of this support, I think it is still valid but in a less precise way than he makes out. In that less precise form I do not think his notion either militates against or confirms the notion I have put forward in my essay.

J. C. Maxwell in *The Pseudo-Problem of 'Comus'* (*Cambridge Journal*, i, pp. 376–80) thinks that I complicate unnecessarily, that there is no reference to marriage, and that too much is made of the doctrine of virginity in the poem. Of course it is impossible to *prove* a reference to marriage. All one can do is to repeat that Milton introduced into the 1637 version in a very emphatic place, and in that place called special attention to ('List, mortals, if your ears be true'), an unmistakable allusion to a famous canto of Spenser in which the two dominant themes are the virtuous bounty of nature and the congruence with it of human marriage. Further, Milton knew and admired Spenser and considered himself Spenser's successor. It is unlikely that Milton should have ignored one of the two prime significances of the passage to which he alludes.

As to the doctrine of virginity Maxwell thinks that the prime subject is the test not of virginity but of virtue. It is quite true that when the Attendant Spirit presents the young people to their parents he praises their general steadfastness and that the last lines of all praise virtue. But there has been no question of the brothers' virginity, and to mention virginity when they and their sister are presented would be inept, while to generalize a narrower theme at the end is a matter of politeness to the audience, of making the special theme apply to them all. The central theme is the test of virginity. When Comus praises the Lady's beauty and suggests that it has a meaning, and then presses her to drink, are we to conclude that she looked, in his opinion, as if her destiny was merely to get drunk? It is a virgin, Sabrina (and her virginity is stressed), who has to release the Lady. And behind Sabrina there is Fletcher's *Faithful Shepherdess*, where the theme of virginity and its potency is prominent—even to a distressing degree. In one passage Maxwell advances to show that *virtue* is the main theme (the Elder Brother's 'Vertue may be assail'd, but never hurt', line 589), the word, in the context, bears its possible restricted sense of chastity as well as its more general sense. And why, after all, should Milton not have used the trial of virginity for his central theme? Quite apart from the *Faithful Shepherdess*, its ancestry goes back to the legends of the Saints, while for its dramatic exploitation there are the plays of Roswitha.

Maxwell is of course right in bringing forward the danger of reading too much into a poem, one of the besetting vices of contemporary criticism. But scepticism too may have its own peculiar dangers.

Kenneth Muir touched on the subject of this essay in *Penguin New Writing*, 24, pp. 141–3. He wrote: 'Milton chose neither side in the debate; the licence of Comus is contrasted with the limitations of the Lady.'

D. C. Allen's noteworthy article on *Comus* in *English Literary History*, xvi, 104–19, did not reach me till this book was in proof. Since it concerns the success or failure of the total poem and not the more restricted theme of the poem's action, it is really outside the scope of my paper.

The Christ of Paradise Regained and the Renaissance Heroic Tradition

IN his excellent article on the above topic in *Studies in Philology*[1] Merritt Y. Hughes has proved that the substance of *Paradise Regained* is far less private to Milton and far less purely stoical than many recent critics have allowed. If Milton starved his hero of positive action he had the precedent of the medieval romance and of Catholic theology. Further he was in a pure Renaissance tradition when in his hero Milton gave his christianized version of Aristotle's magnanimous man. The renunciation of glory, so important a topic in *Paradise Regained*, was a matter both of traditional interest and very much alive in Milton's own day. Milton's Christ as exemplary hero is of the central Renaissance type; and as the 'perfect shape' of virtue, fulfils the requirements of Protestant neo-platonism. The above contentions, taken together, make a formidable and convincing case for *Paradise Regained* having for its substance things that were quite public to the intellectual audience of its day. Milton's Christ stands out as a great traditional figure.

But, though I admit the validity of most of Hughes's theses, I hesitate to draw from them the full conclusion he favours. In proving the public character of Milton's substance he would deny certain inferences drawn from the poem about the nature of Milton's private thoughts at the time. Now, I maintain that such a proof *need* not produce this further result. For there is nothing to prevent a poet's revealing, by the way he uses public material, a phase of his own personal development. Nor of course does such a revelation prevent his expressing simultaneously thoughts that find an echo in every bosom. The traditional, the public material available for poets resembles the common microbes that infest the

[1] xxxv (1938), 254–277.

atmosphere. They are there all the time, but the individual constitution has its own way of dealing with them. Hughes has proved that the germ of *Paradise Regained* is of the nature of the measles, not of some remote tropical disease, but it does not follow that Milton's getting measles just then was not for him an important private experience. And it is when Hughes writes of the processes of Milton's mind that I find I sometimes disagree.

'From the time when he wrote *Church Government,*' writes Hughes (pp. 264–5), 'until he completed *Paradise Regained* Milton must have been concerned over the conflict of the contemplative with the active ideal and in its possible solution by some "heroic" spirit, in art, if not in life.' With this general idea I agree, but not with the form Hughes makes this conflict take in Milton's mind during his life.

To begin with, the conflict and its solution may have filled Milton's mind a good deal earlier than 1642. Already in his three poems on Christ's nativity, circumcision, and passion he had indicated the spheres of activity and of resignation and the perfect union of those qualities in a heroic Christ. The infant Christ in the *Nativity Ode* is an active principle silencing the oracles and routing the heathen gods. In the *Passion* Christ is one who *freely*, that is after meditation, chose to undergo tribulations and who emerges as the perfect hero.

> For now to sorrow must I tune my song,
> And set my Harpe to notes of saddest wo,
> Which on our dearest Lord did sease er'e long,
> Dangers, and snares, and wrongs, and worse then so,
> Which he for us did freely undergo.
> > Most perfect *Heroe*, try'd in heaviest plight
> Of labours huge and hard, too hard for human wight.

Hughes has already in his edition of Milton pointed to the significance of the 'labours' in this passage. There is a reference to Hercules, which at once links *The Passion* with the climax of *Paradise Regained* (iv, 562–8), where Christ and Satan are compared to Hercules and Antaeus and with the transcendental interpretations of the Hercules myth, common in the Renaissance. It would of course be absurd to stress these three early poems of Milton too hard, but they suggest that he was already occupied with the theme of activity and contemplation and that the balance between the two was even.

It would take far too long to trace the emergence of this theme in the course of Milton's work: it shows itself constantly. Indeed it is one of his master-themes, felt through every fibre of his nature. And the final conclusion is ever the same: that, for all his furious urge to activity, contemplation, the purged and settled state of mind, is ever the condition on which activity is legitimate. The urge to activity rewarded by glory is seen at its height in the *Seventh Prolusion* and in *Lycidas* but made all the more wonderful by its subordination to humility and contemplation.

When Milton came to consider his *Arthuriad*, he put the element of activity well to the fore.

> Si quando indigenas revocabo in carmina reges,[1]
> Arturumque etiam sub terris bella moventem;
> Aut dicam invictae sociali foedere mensae
> Magnanimos Heroas, et (O modo spiritus ad sit)
> Frangam Saxonicas Britonum sub Marte phalanges.
> *(Mansus, 80–4)*

True, the heroes of the Round Table are *magnanimi*, they must realize that ideal of Christian Aristotelian magnanimity Hughes describes so well, but the emphasis is on the action of war.

We now come to a phase of Milton's life where, it seems to me, the usual balance between action and contemplation was upset. I mean the period of the tracts against the Bishops, when Milton's sight was dazzled by the vision of a truly regenerate homeland. Hughes (pp. 158–9) seems to me to force things when he sees a connection between a heroic, otherworldly Christ in *Reason of Church Government* and the Christ of *Paradise Regained*. He writes

[1] 'If ever I shall bring back to my verse our native kings and Arthur planning wars even from below the earth; or shall speak of the high-hearted heroes, the unconquered company of the Round Table, and (may the spirit help) I shall break the Saxon bands under the battling of the Britons.'

> Though the pamphlet professed what Milton at the time of writing took to be his sincere loyalty to 'the free and untutored' monarch that Charles I was perhaps destined to become, its real devotion was to 'Our Saviour Christ', whom 'Pilate heard once . . . professing that "his Kingdom was not of this world".'

Surely, this is to give the wrong turn to the passage of Milton[1] here referred to. Milton mentions Christ's otherworldliness not as a main theme but as a subordinate point in a discussion of the usefulness of bishops to the monarchy.

Milton's point is that primitive pastors (unlike bishops) are innocuous to the monarchy because of the unworldliness they have derived from Christ. The unworldliness of Christ is, in this context, of scant importance to Milton compared with his eagerness to get busy with destroying the episcopacy. And even the magnificent apostrophe of Christ at the beginning of the pamphlet occupies but a portion of the opening sentence, which ends,

> I do not know of any thing more worthy to take up the whole passion of pitty on the one side, and joy on the other: then to consider first, the foule and sudden corruption, and then after many a tedious age, the long-deferr'd but much more wonderfull and happy reformation of the *Church* in these latter dayes.

The apostrophe indeed stands to the body of the pamphlet rather as a perfunctory grace stands to the gastric earnestness of a banquet. Not that Milton quite omitted from this, his most active pamphlet, the prerequisite of patience and the power to sit still. Indeed in one of his most fervent passages, his exhortation of England and Scotland not to be separated,[2] he explicitly associates those virtues with the heroic.

> Nor shall the *wisdome*, the *moderation*, the *Christian pietie*, the *Constancy* of our Nobility and Commons of *England* be ever forgotten, whose calme and temperat connivence could sit still, and smile out the stormy bluster of men more audacious and precipitant, then of solid and deep reach. . . . Nor must the *Patience*, the *Fortitude*, the firme *Obedience* of the Nobles and

[1] iii, 42.
[2] iii, 60–1.

People of *Scotland* striving against manifold Provocations, nor must their sincere and moderate proceedings hitherto, be un-remember'd, to the shamefull Conviction of all their Detractors. Goe on both hand in hand, O Nations never to be disunited be the *Praise* and *Heroick Song* of all Posterity.

Now that, on the face of it, is close to the introduction of Book Nine of *Paradise Lost* with its exaltation of 'the better fortitude of Patience and Heroic Martyrdom' and to the whole tenor of *Paradise Regained*. But it would be an error to judge *Reason of Church Government* by a few artificially isolated passages. And the overwhelmingly strong bent of that pamphlet is the excited confidence in immediate action. 'Speedy and vehement were the reformations of all the good Kings of Judah,' Milton exclaims, and, 'Let us not dally with God when he offers us a full blessing.' That is the spirit of the pamphlet, backed by a compact mass of historical precedents. And the God whom Milton invokes at the close is not *Christus patiens* but the God who scattered the ships of the Spanish Armada.

How Milton turned against this over-emphasis on action I have described elsewhere[1]; nor do I think that this process is chimerical because it corresponds to a trend of feeling already familiar in the Middle Ages. I am grateful to Hughes for pointing to a *post hoc*, but a *post hoc* need not imply a *propter hoc*. When at the beginning of the ninth book of *Paradise Lost* Milton repudiated as the supreme epic subject

> the wrauth
> Of stern *Achilles* on his foe pursu'd
> Thrice fugitive about *Troy* wall; or rage
> Of Turnus for Lavinia disespous'd,

he may not have done anything original, but he may have expressed a principal development in his own mental life.

Before going on to *Paradise Regained* I must question Hughes's contention (p. 264) that from the autobiographical passage in *Reason of Church Government* it is likely that Milton

[1] *The Miltonic Setting*, 198–201.

was actually planning a short epic on the model of *Job* with Job or Christ for hero. Hughes writes (p. 264),

> Milton was embarrassed, he said, by a doubt whether any 'King or Knight, before the conquest, might be chosen in whom to lay the pattern of a Christian hero'. Already, perhaps, his reading of British history had made him feel that the true Arthur fell far short of his imaginary namesake in *The Faerie Queene*.

Hughes and I seem to read this passage of Milton in different senses. But surely Milton does not hint at the slightest embarrassment, and the alternatives he is seriously concerned with and between which he has to choose are epic, tragedy, and lyric. The classical and Hebrew forms of the epic are distinguished in a mere aside, not as if they were objects of immediate choice. There does not seem to me the slightest evidence that Milton was then 'planning the framework of very much of the *Paradise Regained* that we know'.

But even if he was, that should not deter us from judging *Paradise Regained*, not by any preconception which the historical setting of its subject-matter may appear to suggest, but by the effect the poem has on us as a whole. Even if Milton planned a *Paradise Regained* in 1642, it does not follow that the poem, had he written it then, would in essentials have been at all the same poem as the *Paradise Regained* we actually have. The situation is this. Hughes has proved that *Paradise Regained* has for its hero a richly traditional figure and that it deals with a theme—the relation between action and contemplation—which had long been present in Milton's mind. Does it then necessarily follow that it is false to detect in the poem any element, private as it were to this poem, which reflects a state of mind in Milton different from what we find in *Paradise Lost* or *Samson Agonistes*?

Much as I welcome Hughes's establishment of the 'public' character of Milton's material in *Paradise Regained*, I find on re-reading the poem in the light of his article that I still cling to my conviction that Milton's spirit is not working with quite its full freedom. And I find in the poem exactly the opposite of what I find in *Reformation in England*. In the prose work the emphasis is, for Milton, unduly on action; in *Paradise Regained* unduly on the passive virtues. I can best explain what I mean by comparing Adam's last speech in *Paradise Lost* (xii, 553–73) with Christ's repudiation of wordly culture in *Paradise Regained* (iv, 286–364). In Adam's speech the resignation is utter and there is no repining. When he speaks of 'subverting . . . worldly wise by simply meek', there is no pain and no anger. And behind the utter emptying of the self of ambition is the assurance of those 'deeds to thy knowledge answerable' of which Michael speaks a few lines lower down. But in Christ's speech there is a tone of anger, for which I fail to make dramatic propriety or historical precedent account. Christ speaks superbly, but somehow he protests too much. And some unusual explanation seems required.

It is a great advantage to have *Paradise Regained* given a truer historical setting; yet the dignity of that setting must not be allowed to persuade us that the poem expresses the richness of Milton's mind as successfully as *Lycidas* or *Paradise Lost* or *Samson Agonistes*.

Milton's Private Correspondence and Academic Exercises

1. *The Text*

IN 1674, the year of Milton's death, Brabazon Aylmer, a printer of Cornhill, sought permission of the authorities to publish the public and private correspondence of Milton. To the private correspondence there was no objection, but the public correspondence consisted of letters of State, composed by Milton on behalf of the Cromwellian Government for despatch to the various courts of Europe. The time had not yet come when anything to do with Cromwell could be taken calmly, and permission to publish Milton's public correspondence was denied. Thereupon the printer solicited Milton for something to take its place. Milton discovered in his papers some of the Latin exercises or disputations he had composed at Cambridge to satisfy the requirements for his degrees. The printer accepted these and published them along with Milton's private letters in a duodecimo volume.

This volume is the sole authority for the text of very nearly all the letters and of all the exercises. Besides being badly punctuated it contains not a few misprints but it is not more inaccurate than one would expect a printed Latin book dated 1674 to be. Textually, therefore, it is the original edition only that counts.

2. *Milton's Private Correspondence*

If the reader expects to find in Milton's letters the sort of thing that he finds in those of Howell or Lamb or Keats, he will be disappointed. He will also be misjudging Milton's intention. For Milton treated the Latin letter as a serious set form of composition, on which a good deal of trouble had to be expended. It was something that served among other things to exhibit the writer's command over the Latin language. So it is that he apologizes for possible deficiencies in a passage like the following:

> I write this in London, among the distractions of the town, not, as usual, surrounded by books. So if anything in this letter fails to please you or to fulfil your expectations, it shall be made good in another, upon which more pains have been bestowed, as soon as I return to the haunts of the Muses.

Taking into account this presumption of rhetoric in Milton's letters, we can easily explain certain of their features. First, the long letters are invariably better than the short. Many of the best letter-writers charm us most when they have least to say. Not so Milton. Instead of allowing his fancy to fill the vacuum, he merely elaborates a few compliments or a few excuses for not having written before; and as the rhetorical virtuosity of such elaboration has ceased to charm, part of the reason for these letters' existence has disappeared. On the other hand, when Milton has matter to express and must needs write at length, he can write with urbanity or nobility: his rhetoric has found a function and we can enjoy it. Most of the long letters are good. Secondly, rhetoric helps to explain a tone of formality which in some of the letters is rather distressing. In writing to a distinguished foreigner, Milton uses a mode of elegant hyperbole which is superbly appropriate. We at once understand why he had such a success in Italy. But when he is nearly as formal, without being so complimentary, in writing to an old pupil, our first thoughts are that Milton must have been rather disagreeable. Take these sentences from the thirtieth letter, to Richard Jones:

> On no account allow yourself to imagine that I measure your gratitude (if indeed you owe me any) by the regularity of your letters. You can best prove your gratitude to me by showing the results of those services of mine to you, of which you speak, not so much in the frequency of your letters as in your steady devotion to noble pursuits and in the merits of your conduct.

This, we say, is tall stuff, little calculated to endear Milton to his correspondent. Yet, if we remember the presumption of rhetoric, we may somewhat revise our opinions. To write tall stuff was part of the game. Milton apparently had nothing particular to say to Jones; so he played the game by filling out with a little rhetorical moralizing.

As examples of literary skill that still retains its charm, I would cite letters twelve and twenty-three. Philaras, to whom the first of these is addressed, by birth an Athenian, educated in Italy, and a distinguished scholar and diplomat, had admired Milton's *Defence of the English People* against Salmasius and had written to beg him to use his eloquence in the cause of freeing the Greeks from Turkish rule. It is pretty plain from Milton's letter that he had no wish to accede to Philaras's request, because he thought the Greeks of his time incapable of bearing the responsibilities of liberty. Yet he succeeds in conveying this unpleasant opinion with the most perfect urbanity, so delicately indeed that perhaps Philaras never consciously disentangled it from its florid setting. (Milton, it may be remembered, somehow succeeded in including urbanity among the virtues extracted from Scripture in the *De Doctrina Christiana*.) More than half the letter consists of compliments: some to Philaras, some to himself for having earned the praise of anyone so distinguished as Philaras, a man in whom all the lost virtues of ancient Greece have been revived. The tone is perfect: it has a kind of baroque gravity like that of a good heroic play; imperturbably and solemnly exaggerated and yet critically conscious of the exaggeration. Then Milton turns to the business in hand. Could anything be more noble, more in keeping with classical precedent, than to urge Europe to attempt the emancipation of Greece? Yet what about the Greeks themselves? Should not *they* be first encouraged to emulate their ancestors? But you, Philaras, are the only person who can effect this. Doubtless *you* can do it; and when once it is done, the Greeks will be sufficient to themselves and other nations will stand by the Greeks. Nothing could be neater than the way Milton turns the tables on his correspondent.

The other letter, to Henry de Brass, is much simpler, containing no irony. It is a little essay on the nature of History and on Sallust as a historian. It is a beautiful piece of single-minded ardour culminating in the very Miltonic sentiment that only a man who is himself noble is qualified to write the actions of noble men.

> One who would be a worthy historian of worthy deeds must possess as noble a spirit and as much practical experience as the hero of the action himself, in order that he may be able to comprehend and measure even the greatest of these actions on equal terms.

Such are some of Milton's qualities as a writer of letters. Something remains to be said of the letters, not as letters, but as documents telling us things about Milton. The intervals at which they were written are irregular. For instance, Milton left but one letter dating from after the Restoration and as many as twenty written in the decade before. His letters, therefore, cannot furnish us with a steady record of his life and development. Yet up to a point they are very valuable in showing us how he changed: they give us contrasted glimpses of him at different times.

First comes a group of four letters written when Milton was an undergraduate. They are stilted compositions and, except that they show a genuine affection for Young and the younger Gill, to whom they are addressed, they lack the more amiable qualities in Milton's nature which certain passages in the *Prolusions* and the *Nativity Ode* reveal in him at about this time. On the other hand they tell us (see the third letter) that Milton was disappointed with his fellow-undergraduates, disgusted with the superficiality of their learning and with the levity of many of them in becoming theologians with no proper basis of general knowledge. He longs to get away where he can bury himself in solitary and unbroken study. With the dons his standing must have been high, for he tells us that he has supplied one of them with some Latin verses, to be used at a University function.

After a long interval follow three letters of the Horton period. We now see Milton in the midst of the solitary and unbroken study he had longed for in his Cambridge days. The seventh letter, to Diodati, is an invaluable record of Milton's state of mind before he wrote *Lycidas*. In the vehement manner, the somewhat feverish Platonic tone in which he speaks of his friendship with Diodati, we may detect the strain on him of his unremitted studies at Horton, perhaps too of his resolve, deliberately taken five years before, to put off all idea of early marriage.

> Ceres never sought her daughter Proserpine (as the legend tells) with greater ardour than I do this Idea of Beauty, like some image of loveliness; ever pursuing it, by day and by night, in every shape and form ('for many forms there are of things divine') and following close in its footprints as it leads. And so, whensoever I find one who spurns the base opinions of common men, and dares to be, in thought and word and deed, that which the wisest minds throughout the ages have approved; whensoever, I say, I find such a man, to him I find myself impelled forthwith to cleave.

But though there may be a sense of strain, ambition and the eagerness to be doing inform the letter.

> What am I thinking about? you ask. So help me God, of immortality. What am I doing? Growing wings and learning to fly.

And the eagerness is not confined to the passages which deal with his ambitions; it has entered the texture of his prose, by now truly eloquent and far superior to the stilted rhetoric of his Cambridge letters.

Two letters survive from Milton's Italian tour, and a third, written years later from England to his Florentine friend, Carlo Dati, may be associated with them. Of all the groups of the letters this gives the fullest, or at least the most agreeable picture of Milton. The formality of style which in the Cambridge letters was unpleasantly cold and stilted now seems to glow with an apt Italianate warmth. The baroque of Lecce has, as it were, supplanted the baroque of Peterhouse chapel. This time the tone is exactly right. The candid delight Milton shows in the Italians' good opinion of him and the generous affection it provoked in return are charmingly expressed. To those who imagine that Milton was a bigoted Protestant it will be surprising to hear him praising Catholics so ardently; in particular Cardinal Barberini, Prime Minister of Rome, protector of the interests of England and Scotland at the Papal Court. And in his letter from England to Dati he is almost pathetically anxious that his anti-Catholic principles should not alienate his Catholic friends. Freedom of speech he must have; but he values his friends to the utmost and cannot relinquish them.

Except the above letter to Dati, none survives between 1639, the year Milton left Italy, and 1652, the period of the Salmasian controversy and the culmination of his blindness. But between the latter year and 1659 come twenty letters, or nearly two-thirds of Milton's total correspondence. In these years Milton was a man of international importance, much visited by foreigners. Aubrey tells us how 'the only induce-ment of severall foreigners that came over into England, was chiefly to see Oliver Protector and Mr. J. Milton'. Fifteen out of the twenty letters are written to foreigners; the other five to former pupils. The contents of the whole group are so miscellaneous that one can make no general comment. The letters to Philaras and Henry de Brass have been mentioned before. The second of these, it may be noted, is only one of several that show Milton's deep love of history. Perhaps the most interesting of all the group is the second letter to Philaras, concerning his blindness. It is famous as describing the symptoms, and has prompted numerous theories as to why Milton went blind. But it illustrates admirably his sen-sitiveness and his courage. He was proud of his own physical fitness, and had no sentimental liking for disease. This pride may help us to estimate the anguish behind his remarks in this letter that his blindness may be causing many to regard him with feelings of contempt. But his courage blazes up higher still. He will not repine at God's will and he bids Philaras farewell 'with as much courage and composure as if I had the eyes of Lynceus'.

The single letter that post-dates the Restoration is of the first interest in revealing how severe the shock of that event must have been. The twenty-ninth letter, written in 1659, had shown Milton still confident in the future of his own political cause. When the blow fell it seems to have extinguished patriotism from his heart.

> The virtue you call statesmanship (but which I would rather have you call loyalty to my country), after captivating me with her fair-sounding name, has, so to speak, almost left me without a country. . . . One's country is wherever it is well with one.

This is the mood of *Paradise Regained*, with which Milton was occupied in the year this letter was written. Christ in that poem had meditated political action, the patriotic work of rescuing Israel from the Roman yoke:

> Yet held it more humane, more heavenly first
> By winning words to conquer willing hearts,
> And make perswasion do the work of fear.

Christ, the perfect man, did not need experience, as Milton did, to learn the futility of staking everything on political action. No letter survives to correspond with the qualified patriotism of *Samson Agonistes*.

Such are some of the features that make Milton's letters important to anyone interested in his life and character. I have left unmentioned many more of those features than I have had room here to discuss.

3. *Milton's Academic Exercises*

Milton's *Prolusions* or *Academic Exercises*, when understood, enrich our knowledge of what Cambridge was like in the years 1625 to 1632. But in order to understand them, a little previous knowledge of conditions in Cambridge is necessary.

The University was at that time in a very flourishing state. The late Dr J. Venn in a book published in 1897 wrote:

> Few persons have adequately realised the commanding position to which the two Universities had thus attained. Absolutely—not relatively merely—the number of graduates in the years about 1625–30 was greater than was ever attained again till

within living memory. When allowance is made for growth of population, it must be frankly admitted that, as far as concerns the number of trained men sent out into the country, the Universities have not yet regained the position they occupied two centuries and a half ago.

The percentage of men, later to become distinguished, who passed through the Universities at that time must have been very high. Still, in numbers Cambridge was less than half what it is now, and its life was incalculably narrower. Undergraduates came up several years younger, and remained in residence twice as long. The numbers passing through Cambridge would therefore be but a quarter of those passing through now. Communication with townsfolk was strenuously discouraged. The men lived close together in college, and their tutors were more like house-masters than like their present-day descendants. It was a small world in which everyone knew everyone else. The range of studies was comparatively narrow. All these conditions must have induced a strong self-centredness, an atmosphere of strenuous 'shop', more usually associated with school than with University.

The discipline, too, at least for those who had not yet got their B.A., was that of a school. Five o'clock was the hour for rising to attend morning chapel. Breakfast was at six. Then followed four hours' work. Dinner was eaten at noon. There was two hours' more work after dinner. Supper at seven was the only other fixture of the day. Though this routine has much of the school about it, the success with which discipline was preserved was very different from what is expected in a school today. Milton in his *Sixth Prolusion* refers to an excursion made by fifty third-year men to Barnwell Field where they appear to have attacked an aqueduct and cut off one of the local water-supplies. This would be but one of many troubles, and complaints reached the Government of the bad state of discipline at this time.

The education in Milton's Cambridge was still founded on the medieval system. The three-and-a-half years spent on gaining the B.A. degree were mainly devoted to Rhetoric, Logic and Metaphysics. Latin and some Greek were taught along with these. Little Mathematics, no History or Science, were included in the course. Everything was supposed to lead up to the *Disputation*, a medieval legacy which took the place of the modern examination. To qualify for a degree every student had from time to time to maintain or to attack a given thesis before an audience, sometimes in his college, sometimes in the Public Schools of the University. It is some of these Exercises or Prolusions on set themes, composed by Milton to satisfy the requirements for his two degrees, that were saved and printed in the 1674 volume.

Narrow as the education may seem, there is a good deal to be said for it, as actually put into practice in Milton's day. First, some latitude was allowed in choice of subject and in the way a subject was treated. History may not have been in the syllabus, yet it seems to have been quite legitimate to work history into a non-historical subject. Thus Milton, called on to defend the very scholastic thesis that 'there are no partial forms in an animal in addition to the whole', works in a long disquisition on the decline of the Roman Empire. Given an enlightened tutor, an undergraduate might be able to indulge his tastes to a large extent. Second, the system of disputation ensured the dons having close contact with their pupils. They took part in the disputations themselves and had to teach their pupils to argue. Some idea of the opportunities a lucky undergraduate might have in Milton's day can be gathered from our knowledge of Joseph Meade, one of the tutors of Christ's. Meade (whose diary is the chief source of the details of Cambridge life in Milton's day) had extended his learning far beyond the range of subjects required for the usual degrees. He was versed in mathematics, modern languages, history, anatomy, and botany. He was also an extremely conscientious tutor, seeing his pupils every evening. This is how his biographer describes these interviews:

In the evening they all came to his chamber to satisfy him that they had performed the task he had set them. The first question he used to propound to every one in his order was: *Quid dubitas?* What doubts have you met in your studies today? For he supposed that to doubt nothing and to understand nothing were verifiable alike. Their doubts being propounded, he resolved their *Quaere's* and so set them upon clear ground to proceed more distinctly. And then having by prayer commended them and their studies to God's protection and blessing, he dismissed them to their lodgings.

Another advantage of the educational system was the actual practice of the public debates; quite apart from the subjects chosen. Habitual attendance at these functions must have sharpened the young men's wits; and a keen audience must have put the speakers on their mettle. Milton's *Prolusions* recreate for us very vividly the consciousness of the audience. We feel that this audience extracted things from Milton's mind which without it would have remained dormant: for example a certain kind of undergraduate wit. The wit may not be very brilliant, but it was good for Milton to have it forced from him. The debate was indeed admirably suited to intensifying and enlivening the narrow, self-centred, but active spirit of early seventeenth-century Cambridge.

This gives the good side of Cambridge education. The bad can be seen from the *Fourth* or *Fifth Prolusions* of Milton. In the former, Milton was called on to maintain that 'in the destruction of any substance there can be no resolution into first matter'. He conducts the argument in the strictest *a priori* manner of medieval philosophy. There is not the least hint that in a scientific matter experiment of any kind should be admitted. This *Prolusion* was typical of a large number, probably the large majority of the University exercises. Whatever value this scholastic method may have had in exercising the brain it implied that Cambridge at that period officially ignored the recent revolution in mathematical and scientific thought. If for Donne the new philosophy had called all in doubt it had entirely failed to penetrate the ears of those in authority at Cambridge. To a young man eager to learn the changes in thought and the new discoveries of science it must have been agony to be kept for years to the treadmill of scholastic logic.

However, though official education was medieval, there existed within the University a party of reformers. Of this party Milton's *Prolusions* are some of the chief evidence. Its inspiration was Francis Bacon. Years before at Cambridge, Bacon had revolted against the methods of teaching, the subservience to Aristotle interpreted medievally. As his earliest biographer said,

> He fell into the dislike of the philosophy of Aristotle; not for the worthlessness of the author, to whom he would ever ascribe high attributes, but for the unfruitfulness of the way.

Three years before Milton's birth, in 1605, Bacon vented this dislike in various passages of the *Advancement of Learning*. The chief subject of University education he condemns as 'vain matter'.

> Surely, like as many substances in nature which are solid do putrify and corrupt into worms, so it is the property of good and sound knowledge to putrify and dissolve into a number of subtile, idle, unwholesome, and (as I may term them) vermiculate questions, which have indeed a kind of quickness and life of spirit, but no soundness of matter or goodness of quality. This kind of degenerate learning did chiefly reign amongst the schoolmen; who having sharp and strong wits, and abundance of leisure, and small variety of reading; but their wits being shut up in the cells of a few authors (chiefly Aristotle their dictator), as their persons were shut up in the cells of monasteries and colleges; and knowing little history, either of nature or time; did out of no great quantity of matter, and infinite agitation of wit, spin out unto us those laborious webs of learning which are extant in their books.

In another place Bacon advocates a complete overhaul of University teaching.

Although the *Advancement of Learning* produced no effect on the academic authorities, Bacon was far too diplomatic to take offence. He took the greatest care to keep on good terms with his University, without ceasing to plead for reform. In 1620 he presented a copy of his *Novum Organum* to the University with a letter, deferential in tone but calling attention to the new method propounded in his work. Again, in 1623 he presented a copy of the *De Argumentis Scientiarum* with the following address:

To the University of Cambridge

The debts of a son, such as I can, I discharge. And what I do myself, I exhort you to do likewise; that is to apply yourselves strenuously to the advancement of the sciences, in modesty of mind to retain liberty of understanding, and not to lay up in a napkin the talent which has been transmitted to you in trust from the ancients. Surely the grace of the divine light will attend and shine upon you, if humbling and submitting Philosophy to Religion you make a legitimate and dexterous use of the keys of the senses; and putting away all zeal of contradiction, each dispute with other as if he were disputing with himself. Farewell.

Zeal of contradiction is plainly a hit at the *Disputation* with its endless raising of objections and counter-objections. Finally, by his will Bacon left money to found a lectureship in history, a subject dear to his heart and completely neglected at Cambridge. Unfortunately, when he died in 1626, the money was found not to be there, and the lectureship never came into being.

The authority of Bacon must have given the reforming party in Cambridge some strength, but that their position was not easy is shown by the following incident. Shortly after Bacon's death, Lord Brooke, himself influenced by Bacon's teaching, founded a lectureship in history at Cambridge. The holder could not be a cleric, and might be a foreigner. As no Englishman could be found qualified for the post (the study of history being at a very low ebb in this country), Isaac Dorislaus of Leyden was appointed. He gave his first lecture in December 1627. Unfortunately some political references in it gave offence to Wren, the High Church Master of Peterhouse. Wren wrote to Laud, who caused Dorislaus to be forbidden to lecture. The unlucky Dutchman, completely innocent of wishing to give offence, made humble apology. He became the centre of contending factions. The ban was removed, reimposed, removed again; but finally Lord Brooke invited him to give up Cambridge and join his household. Dorislaus was glad to accept the offer. It is clear from the incident that a strong section of the authorities were bitterly hostile to any educational reform. And we may guess that the feelings of the reformers were correspondingly violent.

Such were some of the features of the Cambridge which Milton entered in 1625. How Milton reacted to it we know pretty clearly from the *Prolusions*, the letters, a few passages in his Latin poems and later pamphlets, and from one or two remarks by his biographers. His academic record was unimpeachable. 'Was a very hard student in the University,' said Aubrey, 'and performed all his exercises there with very good applause.' But he quarrelled with his first tutor, was for two years at least unpopular with most of his fellow-undergraduates, was actively opposed to the prevailing system of education, and for years afterwards continued to express that opposition. Indeed Cambridge seems to have evoked all those powers of resistance which in a congenial home and at a school where his talents were appreciated had been quiescent. It is possible that the whole trouble arose from his declaring from the first for the Baconians or educational reformers. His tutor Chappell was an exceptionally skilful disputant, presumably a strong believer in the prevailing system. Milton, exasperated at having to spend time on scholastic subtleties when he wanted to study history or mathematics, probably gave his candid opinion on educational methods. And no wonder there was trouble. When, in his *First Prolusion*, he mentions the undergraduates' hostility, he speaks of the rivalry of those who pursue different studies, as if the quarrel was educational rather than personal:

> How can I hope for your good-will, when in all this great assembly I encounter none but hostile glances, so that my task seems to be to placate the implacable? So provocative of animosity, even in the home of learning, is the rivalry of those who pursue different studies or whose opinions differ concerning the studies they pursue in common. . . . Yet to prevent complete despair, I see here and there, if I do not mistake, some who without a word show clearly by their looks how well they wish me.

It is to the credit both of Cambridge and of Milton that these rivalries admitted of reconciliation. Milton was transferred to a more congenial tutor; and in the *Sixth Prolusion*, or *Vacation Exercise*, he refers most generously to his late opponents, now reconciled to him. The fact is that though freedom of speech was a necessity of his nature, he was singularly free from personal rancour, having a sweetness of disposition difficult at first sight to reconcile with the violence of some of his utterances. And freedom of speech the authorities were wise enough to allow him, for the *Third Prolusion* is a direct attack on the Scholastic Philosophy, indeed on the whole educational system of Cambridge.

The date of this composition is uncertain, but cannot be very far removed from the time when, as described above, Dorislaus retired from Cambridge owing to the action of Laud. As Milton expressly speaks of the importance of history, his speech must have stirred up feeling pretty effectively. It is interesting to note that two or three years after this *Prolusion* a certain Nicholas Ganning, Fellow of Corpus, was 'objected to as a disputant at the Commencement of 1631 on the ground that he railed against school divinity, whereas King James and King Charles commanded young students in divinity to begin with Lombard and Aquinas'. In tone Milton's *Prolusion* is entirely uncompromising. It is less an argument than a glowing poetical denunciation of scholastic philosophy and a panegyric of the new studies advocated by Bacon. This is how he describes the studies he hates:

> When I go through these empty quibbles as I often must, against my will, it seems to me as if I were forcing my way through rough and rocky wastes, desolate wildernesses, and precipitous mountain gorges. And so it is not likely that the dainty and elegant Muses preside over these ragged and tattered studies, or consent to be the patrons of their maudlin partisans; and I cannot believe that there was ever a place for them on Parnassus unless it were some waste corner at the very foot of the mountain, some spot with naught to commend it, tangled and matted with thorns and brambles, overgrown with thistles and nettles, remote from the dances and company of the goddesses, where no laurels grow nor flowers bloom, and to which the sound of Apollo's lyre can never penetrate.

And when he praises the studies of his choice, the prose rises to a pitch of enthusiasm unequalled by any of his verse written at that date:

> But how much better were it, gentlemen, and how much more consonant with your dignity, now to let your eyes wander as it were over all the lands depicted on the map, and to behold the places trodden by the heroes of old, to range over the regions made famous by wars, by triumphs, and even by the tales of poets of renown, now to traverse the stormy Adriatic, now to climb unharmed the slopes of fiery Etna, then to spy out the customs of mankind and those states which are well-ordered; next to seek out and explore the nature of all living creatures, and after that to turn your attention to the secret virtues of stones and herbs. And do not shrink from taking your flight into the skies and gazing upon the manifold shapes of the clouds, the mighty piles of snow, and the source of the dews of morning; then inspect the coffers wherein the hail is stored and examine the arsenals of the thunderbolts. And do not let the intent of Jupiter or of Nature elude you, when a huge and fearful comet threatens to set the heavens aflame, nor let the smallest star escape you of all the myriads which are scattered and strewn between the poles: yes, even follow close upon the sun in all his journeys, and ask account of time itself and demand the reckoning of its eternal passage.

Even when forced to engage in the scholastic game he does not give up the battle. In the *Fourth Prolusion* he punctuates his dialectic with the remark that he expects he is boring his hearers as he is certainly boring himself. And in the *Fifth Prolusion* he drags a long disquisition on Roman history into a purely scholastic topic—history being one of the subjects he was most anxious should supplant the scholastic philosophy.

Interesting for the history of education as are Milton's attacks on surviving medievalism, they are still more so for what they tell us about himself. They show him, long before his first pamphleteering days at the beginning of the Civil War, as the young reformer, naïvely trusting in a root-and-branch policy, too little suspicious of the insensibility of human nature, and over-confident in the power of rules and institutions to hasten or delay an Age of Gold.

Such then is the way in which Milton reacted to the educational system at Cambridge, as shown especially in the *Third Prolusion*. The other *Prolusions* may now be examined in turn for anything of note they tell us about Milton and his university life.

It is unfortunate that only one of the *Prolusions* is dated. This is the *Vacation Exercise*, delivered in the Long Vacation. The verses *At a Vacation Exercise*, which originally accompanied it, Milton tells us were written when he was nineteen. The exercise dates then in the summer of 1628, Milton's fourth year of college. From the references, quoted above, to academic rivalry, the *First Prolusion* ante-dates the *Vacation Exercise*. The elaborate *Seventh Prolusion*, on Learning and Ignorance, is obviously the maturest of all. It also suggests that Milton had already embarked on the comprehensive voyage of discovery pursued at Horton. Masson is probably right, therefore, in thinking it Milton's last College exercise before he left Cambridge in July 1632. The *Second Prolusion*, on the Harmony of the Spheres, so closely resembles the *Nativity Ode* that I should date it about 1629. For the dates of the other three there is practically no evidence.

The *First Prolusion*, delivered in mid-winter, concerned the appropriate question whether day or night were the more excellent. Milton does not take the subject very seriously; he is half bored. So he plays with it, pads it out elaborately with mythology, indulges in some very youthful jokes, salts it with a little irony, and every now and then, being Milton, cannot prevent his imagination from shooting up. The classical mythology, tedious to most modern readers, must have been appreciated in Milton's day. It was common ground, much of it, to everyone in the audience; it brought with it the delightful sense of familiarity within the academic clique and of strangeness and bafflement without it. It ministered to the vanity of a compact self-centred community. And Milton's classical mythology, well based on the familiar legends to reassure the majority, was in part learned and remote enough to add a flavour of novelty. His jokes are engagingly simple. For instance in discussing the mythologists and what they made of the old legends of the parentage and alliances of Night and Day he says:

> But why they should believe that Phanes, endowed as he was with a wondrous and superhuman beauty, was so much in love with Night, a mere mulatto or silhouette, as even to wish to marry her, seems a problem hopelessly difficult to solve, unless the phenomenal scarcity of females at that time left him no choice.

More engaging, and surprising to those who think Milton incapable of being witty or critical at his own expense, is the sudden bathos after his highest flight. In praising the beauty of Day, he breaks into a poetical[1] description of the dawn. The beasts rejoice, the flowers open their petals to the sun,

> the Earth too decks herself in lovelier robes to honour the Sun's coming, and the clouds, arrayed in garb of every hue, attend the rising god in festive train and long procession.

Mankind in different parts of the world greet the rising sun with pomp and sacrifice—and, to you, gentlemen, of all men is the sun most welcome, for he allows you to get back to your studies so cruelly interrupted by the inclemency of night. It is all very obvious and sweet and simple-minded, but there is considerable pleasure in seeing the redoubtable Milton showing these of all qualities. In sum this *Prolusion*, callow and 'shoppy' though it is, has somehow the quality of charm. It recreates the picture of a very young man, of powerful, ardent, but generous and responsive nature, set in a society which was curiously confined but by no means lacked character and vitality.

In point of sheer craft the *Second Prolusion*, on the harmony of the spheres, is the best of them all. And one may easily miss the craft in the apparent lightness with which the theme is treated. When we read Milton on the music of the spheres we expect sublimity; when we do not find sublimity, we are only too apt to stop expecting anything at all. It is a little difficult

---

[1] For the notion that *L'Allegro* and *Il Penseroso* are related to the *First Prolusion* see the article on those poems in my *Miltonic Setting*.

to realize that Milton was ever capable of treating such a subject wittily or with urbanity. Not that there is no sublimity in the piece, but as in the *First Prolusion*, though here far more elegantly, Milton curbs his flight with bathos and never allows sublimity to spoil the prevailing tone of the whole. There is a second reason, unconnected with the idea of what we expect from Milton, which explains why a modern can easily miss the excellence of this *Prolusion*: the recent decline of rhetoric. Now a condition of rhetoric is the assumption that there resides a virtue in the manner of statement apart from the theme that is being treated; that a theme may merely be the excuse for artifice or ornament or some extrinsic emotion. Many people are willing to allow a corresponding licence in verse: they do not unreservedly agree with Arnold that in poetry 'all depends on the subject. Choose a fitting action, penetrate yourself with the feeling of its situations; this done, everything else will follow'. But the same people who allow something very like rhetoric in verse often cannot be so tolerant of prose. Prose to them exists for what it states, not for any game of artifice. All one can answer is that at certain periods rhetoric has actually meant a great deal to people, and that it should be possible to project oneself into one of those periods. If one can open one's mind to the idea that through a rhetorical framework a variety of experience can be expressed, it is easy to accomplish this feat. And once the feat is accomplished, one hesitates to limit very strictly the range of experience with which rhetoric can cope. Now the *Second Prolusion* of Milton is a piece of rhetoric. It is a short work composed as a prologue to a set disputation; and there is no reason to suppose that Milton at that time was especially interested in the subject. He had to write on this subject, because the subject was there. What matters is the quality of rhetoric with which he treats the subject.

Milton develops his theme as follows. (It must be remembered that a knowledge of what Plato and Aristotle had to say about the music of the spheres was taken for granted in his audience.) He makes it clear that this *Prolusion* is a light prologue to a more rigorous discussion. And he carries out his intention by hovering delightfully between seriousness and banter. First, he says, Pythagoras and Plato never meant their theory of celestial music to be taken literally; it was but a poetical allegory. Aristotle, therefore, was unjust in attacking the literal doctrine. Indeed he deliberately misunderstood it thus in order to gain credit by demolishing the absurdity. And then Milton suddenly turns, and says—supposing for a moment the notion is taken literally, supposing the moving spheres are held to produce actual sounds, can we put up a defence? Perhaps after all the notion *is* true. Certainly nothing but exquisite music could have made the appalling dullness prevailing in the Aristotelian aether tolerable; without music it would have collapsed. Then he turns to deal with the objection that there can be no celestial music because no one on earth has ever heard it; and for a moment he touches on ideas about which he was extremely serious. Under the guise of Greek mythology he speaks of the age of innocence, of Adam, of the Fall, of Christ and possible regeneration. Once, he says, men could hear the music, but since Prometheus brought sin and degradation into the world by the theft of fire, they have fallen too low to apprehend it; in the words of the poet Milton may have had in mind as he wrote,

> But whilst this muddy vesture of decay
> Doth grossly close us in, we cannot hear it.

Pythagoras indeed may have heard it, but he perhaps was really a god. Then Milton adds something of his own. If only our souls were pure and chaste, like Pythagoras's, we could hear this music; and once we heard it, the Age of Gold would return. With a sudden and deliberate fall he ends by saying that his own unmelodious style has been offending against the very music of which he has been speaking. He had better stop.

This coupling of the music of the spheres with the Golden Age clearly associates the *Prolusion* with two verses (13 and 14) of the Hymn in the *Nativity Ode*.

> Ring out ye Crystall sphears,
> Once bless our human ears,

(If ye have power to touch our senses so)
And let your silver chime
Move in melodious time;
    And let the Base of Heav'ns deep Organ blow,
And with your ninefold harmony
Make up full consort to th'Angelike symphony.

For if such holy Song
Enwrap our fancy long,
    Time will run back, and fetch the age of gold,
And speckl'd vanity
Will sicken soon and die,
    And leprous sin will melt from earthly mould,
And Hell it self will pass away,
And leave her dolorous mansions to the peering day.

In the fourth chapter of my *Milton* I have discussed the *Nativity Ode*, noting its variety unique in Milton's poetry, the surprising and successful way in which it blends fancy and imagination. The *Second Prolusion* is of course a much smaller affair than the *Nativity Ode*, but the quality of its rhetoric links it with that poem. Milton blends banter and bathos and sublimity and dreams of a better world, with a success of which later in life he seems to have lost the art.

The *Third Prolusion*, against scholastic philosophy, has been dealt with above. But it is worth noticing how closely in its enthusiasm for learning it resembles Milton's greater *Prolusion*, the seventh. The enthusiasm of its tone belongs to the Renaissance. Milton speaks of letting the mind go out on adventures:

Let not your mind rest content to be bounded and cabined by the limits which encompass the earth, but let it wander beyond the confines of the world.

He was to repeat the idea later: in *Areopagitica*, 'minds that can wander beyond limit and satiety,' and in the second book of *Paradise Lost*, 'thoughts that wander through eternity'. Milton's enthusiasm in the *Third Prolusion* is much like that of the youthful Marlowe. It is quite possible that in the above passages he was remembering unconsciously a famous passage from *Tamburlaine*:

> Nature, that fram'd us of four elements,
> Warring within our breasts for regiment,
> Doth teach us all to have aspiring minds:
> Our souls, whose faculties can comprehend
> The wondrous architecture of the world,
> And measure every wand'ring planet's course,
> Still climbing after knowledge infinite,
> And always moving as the restless spheres,
> Wills us to wear ourselves, and never rest.

Of the two next *Prolusions*, the rigidly scholastic disputations, I am not competent to speak. Only an expert in medieval philosophy could find them interesting in themselves or judge of their merits as philosophical exercises. But they have a secondary interest in showing us the sort of stuff Milton was attacking and in proving that his hostility was not due to his being unable to cope with the studies he attacked.

The *Sixth Prolusion*, or *Vacation Exercise*, was delivered after the end of the summer term of 1628. It is an elaborately comic entertainment celebrating the breakup of the year's serious studies. That Milton was chosen to give it—before almost the entire University, as he tells us—proves that he was by this time a popular and respected person. It consists of three parts. First an address on the theme that 'sportive exercises on occasion are not inconsistent with philosophical studies'. This is a kind of defence of the second part, which is entirely comic, a medley of hyperbole, topical references and some bawdry. At the end of this part Milton introduces himself as the Father of the ten Aristotelian Predicaments and proceeds to the third part, the *Lines at a Vacation Exercise*, hitherto printed separately among the poems. It is a fragment of a kind of scholastic masque, with Milton as Ens, father of the ten Predicaments. The verses were supplemented by prose, presumably not written by Milton, which has not survived.

What makes the *Sixth Prolusion* so strange a production is that Milton was doing something for which he was quite unfitted yet of which through sheer force of will he made something of a success. It is plain that he took on the task not of his own choice but simply to oblige. He candidly admits that he has no aptitude for exuberant fun, and guards himself from misunderstanding by saying that any smut in which he indulges will spring not from himself but from the exigencies of the occasion. In the first part he fills up his deficiency in humorous matter by confiding to his audience with typical candour and simple-mindedness his own plans for self-education. Then he praises the eminence of his audience with the tallest rhetorical tautology. In a way he is noble and generous; but the tone is wrong, he strains himself too much for urbanity, and deviates into mere youthful bombast. Finally he defends mirth with an overwhelming series of arguments from reason, experience, and ancient example, all in the best Renaissance tradition. In a way Milton makes a hopeless mess of his task: nothing could be less fitting to a comic occasion than this mixture of redundant compliment and rhetorical argumentation. Yet for all that, as we read, we get caught up by the author's vitality. He forces us to pay him heed, however frigid the convention he makes use of. Moreover a fundamental charm breaks dimly through the superficial heaviness, as the flicker of a smile may transform a solemn face.

In the second part (chiefly famous for its allusion to Milton's nick-name of 'the Lady') there was no escaping the duty of being funny, and Milton plunges headlong into his task. It is a queer, violent, breathless piece of work, in which the author's power of compulsion somehow succeeds in imposing itself on us. When he gets hold of a joke he pushes it with all the strength of his nature to fantastic lengths. For instance two of the college servants at Christ's had names (one of them Sparks) that lent themselves to jokes about fires; and flames, sparks, and embers fill several pages. And there is little doubt that the speaker by sheer vitality left his audience no choice but to respond.

It is easy to see why Milton added the verses. Only too conscious that in his comic prose he was doing something for which he had no aptitude, pride must have prompted him to give his audience a taste of what he could do; and he urges his verse to mount when he speaks of the 'graver subjects' on which he would like to use it,

> Such where the deep transported mind may soare
> Above the wheeling poles, and at Heav'ns dore
> Look in, and see each blissful Deitie
> How he before the thunderous throne doth lie,
> Listening to what unshorn *Apollo* sings
> To th'touch of golden wires, while *Hebe* brings
> Immortal Nectar to her Kingly Sire.

As a whole, then, the *Vacation Exercise* is a strange medley of crudity, charm, simple-mindedness and power. When we remember that its author was but nineteen, it is an impressive production. Further it gives, even more clearly than the *First Prolusion*, a picture of the self-centred active community that Cambridge was in the early years of Charles I.

The *Seventh Prolusion*, on the theme that Learning brings more blessings to men than Ignorance, is in an entirely different class from any of the other *Prolusions*, indeed from anything included in the 1674 volume. It is one of Milton's major works, and that it is almost unknown and has never before been translated in full is a reproach to Miltonic scholarship. It may not be comparable as a work of art to *L'Allegro* and *Il Penseroso* or to *Comus*, but in it Milton speaks out more fully and whole-heartedly than in any writing before *Lycidas*; and unless we give it the fullest heed we are apt to be completely mistaken about what Milton was doing with himself during his years of retirement at Horton. It is in this *Prolusion* that we have a full declaration of the vast ambitions that had possessed Milton and of his intention to promote them by acquiring an equipment of almost universal knowledge. He does not make an explicit declaration, but there is not the slightest doubt that when he speaks generally of the rewards which Learning may hope for, it is his own future that he has also in mind. It is remarkable how many ideas, well known in Milton's later works, are found fully formed or in embryo in this *Prolusion*. Much of the Miltonic philosophy can be gathered from it. Finally it is a superb piece of writing. The Latin has disengaged itself from the trammels of academic rhetoric and rises and falls with the ease and sweep of accomplished eloquence.

I can best point out the important details in the *Prolusion* by giving a brief summary of its argument.

First comes an elaborately argued exordium, a splendid piece of rhetoric, full of the joy of technical accomplishment. Milton, in the confiding manner we should now be used to, tells the audience of his ambition to acquire a full circle of knowledge and of his joys last summer when he retired to the country to study. Back at college he had hoped to continue his work, but he was called on to compose an oration on the advantages of Learning over Ignorance. To comply meant interrupting his course of Learning; and in anger he proposed to defend Ignorance, not subject to these interruptions. But fortune decided otherwise. Ignorance found her champion elsewhere, and Milton decides that he will be like a lover, forcibly separated from his true mistress, Learning, but getting comfort from singing her praises.

His main argument is inspired (if it is necessary to seek specific inspiration) by Plato and Bacon's *Advancement of Learning*. The human mind has in it a divine spark which, like one of the twin horses in the *Phaedrus*, struggles to mount upwards. It is Learning alone that aids this spark to succeed in its object and the mind to triumph over the body. To know the nature of things encourages the soul in its search after God, for when it examines the stars and the other wonders of the world it sees that they were created not for man's benefit but to proclaim God's glory. Perhaps Milton is here echoing a famous passage from Montaigne's *Apology of Raymond de Sebonde*. Compare this of Milton—

> Can we indeed believe, my hearers, that the vast spaces of boundless air are illuminated and adorned with everlasting lights, that these are endowed with such rapidity of motion and pass through such intricate revolutions, merely to serve as a lantern to base and slothful men?

with this from Montaigne (in Florio's version)—

Who hath perswaded man, that this admirable moving of heavens vaults; that the eternal light of these lampes so fiercely rowling over his head; that the horror-moving and continuall motion of this infinite vaste Ocean, were established, and continue so many ages for his commoditie and service?[1]

Milton now raises and settles a possible argument against Learning. How is it that many ignorant men have been virtuous, many learned men vicious? The answer is that the power of learning only shows itself in one who is virtuous as well as learned. Such a man has an influence greater than that possessed by a host of ordinary mortals. Milton in this passage has two ideas at the back of his mind: first, the Renaissance exaltation of the great individual, possibly in its Calvinistic form, the insistence on the Elect; second, his own ambitions. He will make himself one of these great men who influence the destinies of thousands. A passage of this sort (it is one of several in this *Prolusion*) has an important bearing on the nature of Milton's prose works. It is usually thought that Milton's early ambition was to be a poet; that the prose works were undertaken entirely against his will, and that without the special occasions that evoked them they would not have been written. But this *Prolusion* suggests that Milton's ambitions were very comprehensive. He wished to sway men, to be a great teacher. Now at the end of the autobiographical passage in the *Defensio Secunda* he speaks of his earlier pamphlets as if they were a systematic exposition of the idea of liberty in the various spheres of life. And though actually these pamphlets were occasioned by specific political or domestic events, there is no reason to doubt Milton's statement that they embody a coherent mass of teaching on which he had pondered long before he committed it to print.

[1] Here is another possible link between Montaigne and Milton. Phillips records that when Milton was living in London shortly after his return from Italy he would punctuate his austere and frugal life once in three weeks or a month with a gaudy-day. Was he acting on this passage from Montaigne (*Essais*, ii, 2, *De l'Yvrognerie*)? 'J'ay ouy dire à Silvius, excellent médicin de Paris, que, pour garder que les forces de nostre estomac ne s'aparessent, il est bon, une fois le mois, les esveiller par cet excez, et les picquer pour les garder de s'engourdir.' But more probably Milton believed in the moral rather than the physical benefits of an occasional gaudy-day.

It seems to me quite clear that, in this *Seventh Prolusion*, Milton is thinking of ambitions that were realized in the prose works quite as much as of those that were realized in *Paradise Lost*.

Next, Milton argues that if all learning is banished, stark savagery must prevail. And to support his thesis he gives a gross travesty (in the Renaissance-Protestant manner) of the conditions of life in the Middle Ages. Then he discusses the relation of the Intellect and the Will. It is true that though the Intellect is the seat of Learning, the Will is the parent of virtue. Yet the Intellect is the superior, for only by nourishment from the Intellect can the Will exercise its proper function. The Will is the agent, the Intellect the originator.

Having spoken generally, Milton deals with the influence of Learning on ordinary life; first private, then public. This is the most important passage in the *Prolusion*. It is here that all Milton's ardour for knowledge and the power of his personal ambitions break out. The extraordinary thing is that the whole spirit of this passage is not that of the soberer Neo-classic pursuit of detailed scientific knowledge but of the boundless expectations of the full Renaissance. Milton indeed writes like Marlowe, and as if the passionate disillusion which blighted those high hopes in the early seventeenth century had never existed. Past such a work as Donne's *Anniversaries*, past Webster with such sentiments as—

> Thou art happy, that thou hast not understanding
> To know thy misery: For all our wit
> And reading, brings us to a truer sense
> Of Sorrow—

Milton goes back and recaptures the simple expansive faith in the joys of knowledge, the insatiable appetite of the human mind, to be found in Marlowe and Sidney. He enumerates the transcendent prizes that reward Learning. It fortifies the mind against death. It promotes the highest form of friendship, even though it may rob a man of the superficial social graces. (Milton, it must be remembered, was never anti-social, and he consistently exalted the political as well as the individual virtues. Here he says that 'the chief part of human happiness is derived from the society of one's fellows and the formation of friendships'.) Then he launches out into a wonderful account of the universal cycle of knowledge, which he has confessed he is ambitious to complete. It goes through all the phenomena of the natural world to the soul of man and the nature of angels and demons. When this universal cycle of knowledge has been compassed, the spirit of man breaks from its prison-house and tramples on the shifting chances of life. He has become a kind of god, and has dominion over nature.

> So at length, when universal learning has once completed its cycle, the spirit of man, no longer confined within this dark prison-house, will reach out far and wide, till it fills the whole world and the space far beyond with the expansion of its divine greatness. Then at last most of the chances and changes of the world will be so quickly perceived that to him who holds this stronghold of wisdom hardly anything can happen in his life which is unforeseen or fortuitous. He will indeed seem to be one whose rule and dominion the stars obey, to whose command earth and sea hearken, and whom winds and tempests serve; to whom, lastly, Mother Nature herself has surrendered, as if indeed some god had abdicated the throne of the world and entrusted its rights, laws, and administration to him as governor.

Such was the quality of Milton's ambition. The passage is an amazing outburst of *hubris*, and, one would think, the product of a man inevitably doomed to disaster, obsessed by the illusions of the tragic hero, by the mood in which 'the dove will peck the estridge'. It seems incredible that a man who thought so overweeningly should have survived the humiliation of his first marriage—all his learning powerless to prevent an elementary social blunder—and the disappointment of the political hopes with which he had identified all his personal ambitions. The extraordinary thing about Milton was that somewhere in him was a humility that co-existed with this overweeningness and which saved him when disaster came. To gauge the extremes of Milton's nature, and with them its splendid scope, one should compare this hubristic passage from the *Seventh Prolusion* with Adam's words to Michael in the twelfth book of *Paradise Lost*, after he has witnessed the future history of the world.

> How soon hath thy prediction, Seer blest,
> Measur'd this transient World, the Race of time,
> Till time stand fixt: beyond is all abyss,
> Eternitie, whose end no eye can reach.
> Greatly instructed I shall hence depart,
> Greatly in peace of thought, and have my fill
> Of knowledge, what this vessel can containe;
> Beyond which was my folly to aspire.
> Henceforth I learne, that to obey is best,
> And love with feare the onely God, to walk
> As in his presence, ever to observe
> His providence, and on him sole depend,
> Merciful over all his works, with good
> Still overcoming evil, and by small
> Accomplishing great things, by things deemd weak
> Subverting worldly strong, and worldly wise
> By simply meek.

Here Milton seems utterly to repudiate the appetite for boundless knowledge. Yet we should be as mistaken to accept this repudiation completely as we should be to conclude from the passage in the *Seventh Prolusion* that he was without all reason and humility. Overweeningness and humility, egotism and self-abnegation *always* co-existed in him. That he was ready, if necessary, at any moment to repress his self added power to his ambitions, while his humilities could never have been so impressive without the underlying potentiality of vast expansion.

There is an enthusiastic section on history and geography. History procures for its devotees a kind of retrospective immortality. When, next, Milton describes the honours with which great learning is rewarded he breaks out into fresh enthusiasm and again betrays his own ambitions:

To be the oracle of many nations, to find one's home regarded as a kind of temple, to be a man whom kings and states invite to come to them, whom men from near and far flock to visit, while to others it is a matter for pride if they have but set eyes on him once. These are the rewards of study, these are the prizes which learning can and often does bestow upon her votaries in private life.

It is pleasant to think that this ambition was at least partially fulfilled when Milton's replies to Salmasius had brought him an international fame.

In public life, Milton admits, the rewards of learning are fewer. The learned 'enjoy a kingdom in themselves far more glorious than any earthly dominion'; and they cannot expect the double sway. (So early does Milton mention the idea of the 'paradise within' happier than any external paradise, spoken of near the end of *Paradise Lost*.) Yet the very greatest men, Alexander and Augustus, were philosophers as well as statesmen.

If Ignorance raises the objection to Learning that life is short but Art long, the answer is to deny the proverb. It is our own slackness and our faulty methods of teaching the Arts that are wrong. This passage exhibits Milton's furiously active nature. It also foreshadows the main reason for the Fall in *Paradise Lost*. Eve ate the fruit not so much because she was greedy or disobedient as because she was too slack to realize the importance of the issue. The passage about education contains the germ of his later pamphlet on that subject. If only our methods were right, our trouble would be the opposite of what it is now: far from complaining that life is too short we should learn so much and so quickly that like Alexander we should sigh for more worlds to conquer.

Then he touches on the question of glory. Why labour to gain glory by Learning, says Ignorance, when the world may have but few years to run and there may be too little time left in which men can glorify those to whom glory is due? His answer is the essence of *Lycidas*: 'to have no thought of glory when we do well is above all glory'. Moreover, there is heavenly glory, which matters far more than earthly. Those who have lived sparely and pursued the noble arts will be exalted in heaven.

He ends with an attack on the pleasures of Ignorance.

They are at best but negative, ignoble, and sheltered joys. They are unworthy even of beasts, even of inanimate things. Ignorance would degrade us below the very stocks and stones.

Such in outline is Milton's *Seventh Prolusion*. It may be arrogant in parts, and it may be too rhetorical for modern tastes, but it is one of Milton's major works and one of the noblest expressions of the enthusiasm for Learning that held men's minds in the full tide of the Renaissance.

POSTSCRIPT

On January 24, 1947, Sir John Sheppard gave a charming address on *Milton and his Academic Exercises* at the Royal Institution of Great Britain. In it he differs from my interpretation of the *Prolusions* in two ways. First he allows Milton a lighter and more natural vein of humour than I did. He puts up a good case for the opening of the *First Prolusion* being comic and denies that Milton strained himself over the *Sixth Prolusion*. I prefer not to alter what I wrote earlier, but if I were to rewrite my essay now I should modify it in the light of Dr Sheppard's comments. Opinion has been widely wrong on the whole question of Milton's sense of humour, and it will be some time before it rights itself. Secondly, Dr Sheppard denies Milton's overweeningness in the *Seventh Prolusion*. Milton is no belated Marlowe:

> Milton's belief was not that cleverness or learning, without character, can help us, nor that man's unaided genius, without grace, can give a foretaste of apotheosis. But he does believe that man's capacity and thirst for knowledge are a proof that search into the ways of nature is his bounden duty in the service of God's praise. The intricacy of the great design does not, for him, refute the notion that the whole was made for man; rather, the universe was thus created that man's mind, by searching out its secrets, might become what God intended Man to be.

Certainly Milton was preaching the doctrine of access to God *per speculum creaturarum*, and I may have stressed this side of the *Prolusion* too little. I probably overstressed the overweeningness: nevertheless I do still think that it is there, even if co-existing with very different feelings.

Theology and Emotion in Milton's Poetry

THE revolution in the ways of studying Milton's thought began about the time of the first world war; it became widely known to English readers through Saurat's *Milton Man and Thinker*, published in 1925; and since that date it has kept its course with ever-increasing momentum.[1] By now a great deal has been found out; and one suspects that there is not much more to find. Scholars naturally, in piecing together the pattern of Milton's thought, have used the total body of his work: verse and prose alike. But what most interests the ordinary reader is Milton's best poems; and Milton's thought as it lives and is graded and shaded in those poems, matters more for such a reader than that thought as abstracted from all his works. In this section, thinking of the ordinary reader, I try first to take into account some of the findings of recent scholarship and then to capture and record the emotional stress which Milton gives to the theological side of his thought as it passes into his poetry. It is the kind of thing Arthur Sewell attempted, especially for *Paradise Lost*, in some pages of his *Study in Milton's Christian Doctrine*.[2] The present essay deals with its topic only in the most general way, and it is not in the least comprehensive, being supplementary to the other essays in this book. For instance, I say nothing of the doctrine of humility, having said enough of it on other pages.

One of the best-known incidents in Milton's life is Dryden's visit to him. Aubrey records that Dryden was one of Milton's 'familiar learned acquaintance'. Dryden, Aubrey adds, very much admired him,

> and went to him to have leave to put his *Paradise Lost* into a drama in rhyme. Mr Milton received him civilly and told him he would give him leave to tag his verses.

[1] For a useful summary of recent Milton scholarship see Rajan, 9–21.
[2] London, 1939.

Another account of the same incident adds something to Milton's answer:

> Well, Mr Dryden, says Milton, it seems you have a mind to tag my points, and you have my leave to tag 'em, but some of 'em are so arkward and old-fashioned that I think you had as good leave 'em as you found 'em.

Whether, in speaking of his verses as old-fashioned, Milton meant anything beyond the prosody we cannot tell; but Dryden, when he adapted *Paradise Lost*, brought it up to date in one very important particular. In the eighth book of his poem Milton makes Adam tell Raphael the story of his creation, of the first motion of his consciousness. Adam's first conscious act was to 'turn his wondering eyes toward heaven'. He then scanned the landscape, found he could name the things he saw, asked the natural objects around him if they could tell 'how came I thus, how here', and, answering his own question, concluded:

> Not of my self; by some great Maker then,
> In goodness and in power praeeminent.

At the beginning of the second act of the *State of Innocence and Fall of Man*, Dryden's rhymed opera derived from *Paradise Lost*, Adam is discovered 'as newly created, laid on a bed of moss and flowers, by a rock'. His first words are:

> What am I? or from whence? for that I am
> I know, because I think,

after which he concludes that there is a divine power, of which he is. Now Milton's Adam attains to his belief in a creator through the approved age-long process of seeing him through creation, *per speculum creaturarum*. Dryden's Adam, on the contrary, begins from within himself, from the doctrine that thought proves existence, according to the then novel philosophy of Descartes. From Dryden's point of view not only Milton's prosody but his philosophy was old-fashioned.

Milton, indeed, in spite of his early enthusiasm for Bacon, in spite of his visit to Galileo, in spite of his political radicalism, belonged firmly to the pre-scientific age, when philosophy was still a part of theology. And this was a matter not only of the date when he was born but of his temperament and convictions. While Bacon, and still more Hobbes, include theology in their science and politics, or rather tack it on, Milton traces back every fact and every thought to its origin in the divine. While Bacon is thrilled at the prospect of new discovery in one department of the universe, and while Hobbes rejoices in replacing the supposed fixed moral laws by mere expediency, Milton is content with nothing less than the traditional conception of a perfectly ordered universe with all its parts not only interconnected but properly balanced. Similarly, in the realm of mechanics, Milton could endorse emotionally only the traditional Aristotelian world where all motion implied a mover; a world of abstract space and of movement self-continued unless obstructed, in the new fashion, could only be repellent. Butterfield[1] has put the opposition between the two conceptions in a way very apt to Milton's temperament:

> We have not always brought home to ourselves the peculiar character of that Aristotelian universe in which the things that were in motion had to be accompanied by a mover all the time. A universe constructed on the mechanics of Aristotle had the door half-way open for spirits already; it was a universe in which unseen hands had to be in constant operation, and sublime Intelligences had to roll the planetary spheres around. Alternatively, bodies had to be endowed with souls and aspirations, with a 'disposition' to certain kinds of motion, so that matter itself seemed to possess mystical qualities. The modern law of inertia, the modern theory of motion, is the great factor which in the seventeenth century helped to drive the spirits out of the world and opened the way to a universe that ran like a piece of clockwork.

The same refusal to split theology from any department of life appears in Milton's politics. In the ends he pursued Milton was close to the extreme reformers, the Levellers, but those ends were not a political programme which, once

[1] *The Origins of Modern Science* (London, 1949), 7.

adopted, was just to be pushed through; they were ends vitally connected with the whole body of his thought. This resolution to think organically (after his own lights), to refuse to departmentalize religion, brought its penalty, for

> the future did not belong to those who strove with him to combine freedom of thought and imagination with a strict walk with God, but to those who separated the spiritual and the natural and thereby released the latter to follow its own untrammelled courses, either scientifically according to the prophecy of Bacon, or politically according to the programme of the Levellers. Such a division Milton refused to accept. It seemed to him to release undisciplined forces which might carry with them their own ruin.[1]

This same trend of mind allied Milton with Hooker and the traditionalists, and with the Cambridge Platonists, against Hobbes, in the matter of ethics. Milton insisted on an organic connection between God and his universe. The nature of good and evil is consonant with God and cannot be other than it is. God cannot change the law of nature. In the words of Cudworth, Milton believed *boni et mali moralis naturas esse prorsus immutabiles nec revera ab ipsius Dei arbitrio pendere.*[2] Hobbes, on the other hand, following a minority opinion that goes back to Scotus, thought that good and bad are such not in themselves but because God has arbitrarily ordained them so. He could have made the universe other than it is.[3] A universe which is but one of many possible alternatives is less intimately joined to its author than one which issues from the total law of the author's being.

Milton, then, generally accepted the world not of the new science but of the old tradition as epitomized in the first book of Hooker's *Laws of Ecclesiastical Polity*: a world of immutable ethical law, divine beauty, vast diversity (but in spite of diversity perfectly harmonious) and arranged in a system of hierarchies. The mention of Hooker—the opponent of both

[1] Arthur Barker, *Milton and the Puritan Dilemma* (Toronto, 1942), xv.

[2] From a letter. Quoted in E. M. Powicke, *The Cambridge Platonists* (London, 1926), 111.

[3] See Marjorie Nicolson, *Milton and Hobbes* in *Studies in Philology*, 1926, pp. 4–5ff.

Catholicism and Calvinism—makes it wise to insist here that this traditional conception was pretty well exempt from theological controversy before it was undermined by the new science. Though believing in man's utter depravity and in the corruption his fall brought on things outside himself, Calvin did see the glory of God in creation:

> Wherever you turn your eyes, there is no portion of the world, however minute, that does not exhibit at least some sparks of beauty; while it is impossible to contemplate the vast and beautiful fabric as it extends around, without being overwhelmed by the immense weight of glory.[1]

Calvin does not indeed enlarge on this side of theology; his interests lay elsewhere: but he does not counter the traditional view.

Milton's belief in this traditional world picture was, I think, emotionally the most powerful theological element in his poetry, and it finds expression without the least sign of conflict. We know of Milton's love of the *Psalms* and the *Book of Job*; and we may conjecture that he loved them largely because of the many passages that describe the glories of creation and the glory of their creator in them. The liveness of the universe, the bounty of its phenomena, and the beautiful order in which God disposed them were matters of perpetually passionate belief throughout Milton's life. C. S. Lewis[2] has written very well on Milton and Hierarchy, and I need not enlarge on that theme. In my *Miltonic Setting*[3] I wrote of Milton's feeling for the bounty of nature and I do not wish to repeat myself here. But I do wish to attach my remarks there to Milton's theology. Milton did indeed have a natural feeling for fertility, for exuberant life; but that feeling is also a part of a wider feeling for the wonders of a divine universe that was both inconceivably vast and varied and an organism.[4] But I can point to a few passages which

---

[1] *Institutes*, 1. 5. (H. Beveridge's translation, Edinburgh, 1863).

[2] Chapter xi.

[3] 69–72.

[4] My *Elizabethan World Picture* describes the conception and organization of this world, which applies to Milton's as well as to Elizabethan notions. In the pages that follow I may assume some familiarity in the reader with the topics treated in this book.

I did not cite before from *Paradise Lost* which express the charge of emotion in Milton's thoughts on these matters.

First and most obviously there is the hymn of praise Adam and Eve sing before Raphael's visit (v, 153–208). It is mainly a paraphrase of the 148th Psalm, and its very simplicity is Milton's reverent tribute to the original. But it is also a traversing of the Chain of Being from the angels down to the lowest animate existence, with the suggestion that all this marvellous wealth of life makes up an organic whole in praising the creator. The very luminousness of statement, the very ease of utterance, should not deceive us as to the high passion with which the poet speaks. Of a very different kind poetically, less lilting and lyrical, more deliberate and more obviously thoughtful, are Raphael's speeches before and after dinner in the same book: the first explaining why, though an angel, he can eat human food, the second explaining the doctrine of materialism and how it links all existence. These I find the perfection of one kind of metaphysical verse: not Donne's kind where the emotion largely arises from the very fact of argumentation, from the joy of the 'works', but Lucretius's where the emotion refers to the subject explained, where the author is just passionately convinced of the doctrine he expounds. Only Milton's verse moves easily, where Lucretius's, for all the passion, strains and creaks.

> To whom the winged Hierarch repli'd.
> O *Adam*, one Almightie is, from whom
> All things proceed, and up to him return,
> If not deprav'd from good, created all
> Such to perfection, one first matter all,
> Indu'd with various forms, various degrees
> Of substance, and in things that live, of life;
> But more refin'd, more spiritous, and pure,
> As neerer to him plac't or nearer tending
> Each in thir several active Sphears assignd,
> Till body up to spirit work, in bounds
> Proportiond to each kind.

This is indeed angelic speech, and through it Milton conveys without strain or reservátion his entire belief in the unity of creation and the informing power of God that both makes and preserves it. Such unqualified utterance is different from Raphael's hesitant and academic discourse on astronomy (viii, 66–188) and from the combative tone of some of the heavenly colloquy on man's fate and redemption in Book Three. Milton seems genuinely uneasy over the competing astronomical systems, while the combative tone in Heaven argues some unease and division in his mind. But about the world-order Milton speaks with the serenity of strong and abiding conviction.

The passage in which Adam describes Earth's unknown visitors or inhabitants adds something else. It comes in Book Four and after the description of Paradise with its sense of teeming natural life, making us think of the island in the *Tempest* full of sweet sounds and peopled by spirits. But the spirits Adam describes are a more intimate and indispensable part of cosmic perfection than Shakespeare's. Speaking first of the stars Adam says (674):

> These then, though unbeheld in deep of night,
> Shine not in vain, nor think, though men were none,
> That heav'n would want spectators, God want praise;
> Millions of spiritual Creatures walk the Earth
> Unseen, both when we wake, and when we sleep:
> All these with ceaseless praise his works behold
> Both day and night: how often from the steep
> Of echoing Hill or Thicket have we heard
> Celestial voices to the midnight air,
> Sole, or responsive each to others note
> Singing thir great Creator: oft in bands
> While they keep watch, or nightly rounding walk
> With Heav'nly touch of instrumental sounds
> In full harmonic number joind, thir songs
> Divide the night, and lift our thoughts to Heaven.

This passage is not mere embroidery, or an attempt to make Paradise, inevitably limited in some ways, more interesting. It expresses a sense of spirituality very deep in Milton. Whatever his personal opinion, precise or vague, of the angels or of 'middle spirits, Betwixt th'Angelical and Human Kinde', he had intuitions of other modes of life than the obvious ones that meet the eye; and of these his angel-lore is the natural and sincere expression.

Nor does Milton's passion fail when he describes creation itself (vii, 174–550). He does so by direct description, but he ends each day's work with a kind of refrain and there is a lightness of rhythm that is distinctly lyrical. In fact the whole has affinities with the morning hymn of Adam and Eve, and may well be one of Milton's fulfilments of the model of 'those magnific Odes and Hymns' which in *Reason of Church Government* is linked with epic and tragedy as fit for imitation by the dedicated poet. The description wonderfully expresses teeming life but not less the hierarchical idea with the animal creation culminating in man.

Whatever we may think about Milton's direct descriptions of God, he does when writing of God's works make us feel, as no other English poet could, their glorious diversity, their order, their dependence on their creator who made and fosters them by the constant pressure of his inexhaustible power.

The next prime religious matter that lies at the very heart of Milton's emotional life as expressed in his poetry is the joint doctrine of discipline and liberty. And it can be understood only in the light of the matters just discussed. The doctrine was not less personally important to Milton because it was a living issue in Milton's day, fought over by contemporary theologians and politicians, something he just could not have escaped. The vogue of the problem of discipline and liberty merely developed and defined instincts he possessed already. Milton was a man of varied and powerful passions, in whom the joy of living and the sense of life's wonder and bounty were fierce and strong. But with equal strength he believed in order and discipline, for only through order could passion and joy be fulfilled instead of squandered. While servitude consisted in a confined and imposed choice, and licence in an undisciplined and wasteful and hence unfulfilled choice; liberty consisted in freely choosing that maximum of bounty which can only be achieved by the discipline appropriate to the chooser.

For the most general notion of fulfilment through discipline Milton could find sufficient warrant in Aristotle and the traditional world picture, quite apart from that Christian liberty which figured so importantly in Protestant theology. For Aristotle self-fulfilment according to the laws of the self in question was a fundamental doctrine, while the traditional scale of hierarchies implied a vast range of capacities each with its own maximum of experience. Milton had thus a mode of thought ready made, through which to express his own natural instincts in these matters, and he used it. Here is his account of God's bounty to the angels and the discipline they applied to it:

> Forthwith from dance to sweet repast they turn
> Desirous, all in Circles as they stood,
> Tables are set, and on a sudden pil'd
> With Angels Food, and rubied Nectar flows:
> In Pearl, in Diamond, and massie Gold
> Fruit of delicious Vines, the growth of Heav'n.
> On flours repos'd, and with fresh flourets crownd,
> They eate, they drink, and in communion sweet
> Quaff immortalitie and joy, secure
> Of surfet, where full measure onely bounds
> Excess, before th'all bounteous King, who showrd
> With copious hand, rejoicing in thir joy.

Here the angels are *desirous*; they have feeling and appetite; and God showered his bounty on them. Their joy was both communal and private. There was no danger of surfeit, and the one limit for all of them was not a partial but the utmost capacity of each. There was no excess, and yet each fulfilled his total power of joy. Adam, in his last dialogue with Michael, says the same thing in another application. He speaks of now having his fill of knowledge, 'what this vessel can contain'.

But the notion of fulfilment through disciplined choice in a vast and lovely field of options is not confined to *Paradise Lost*. It is a master-theme of *Comus*, however puzzling the precise significance of that poem may be:

> How charming is divine Philosophy!
> Not harsh, and crabbed as dull fools suppose,
> But musical as is *Appollo's* lute,
> And a perpetual feast of nectar'd sweets
> Whom no crude surfet reigns.   (476–80.)

And the region to which the Attendant Spirit retires at the end of the poem (like its original, Spenser's garden of Adonis) is one of ordered bounty and fruition, contrasted with the world of Comus not in point of bounty but in point of order and hence fulfilment.

In *Reason of Church Government* Milton rises to one of the highest reaches in his prose to describe the same notion through the celestial dance of the angels.

> Yea the Angels themselves, in whom no disorder is feared . . . are distinguished and quaternioned into their celestial Princedoms and Satrapies, according as God himself hath writ his imperial decrees through the great provinces of heaven. The state also of the blessed in Paradise, though never so perfect, is not therefore left without discipline, whose golden surveying reed marks out and measures every quarter and circuit of new Jerusalem. Yet is it not to be conceived that those eternal effluences of sanctity and love in the glorified Saints should by this means be confined and cloyed with repetition of that which is prescribed, but that our happiness may orb itself into a thousand vagancies of glory and delight, and with a kind of eccentrical equation be as it were an invariable Planet of joy and felicity.[1]

And the special plea for free printing in *Areopagitica* is subordinated to the same great general principle. There Milton speaks of

> the high providence of God, who though he command us temperance, justice, continence, yet powrs out before us ev'n to a profusenes all desirable things, and gives us minds that can wander beyond all limit and satiety.[2]

So long as Milton's thought derives nearly from this general principle and its manifestation in the traditional world

[1] iii, 185–6.
[2] iv, 320.

146

picture it receives unqualified and transparent ratification by his passions. He is certain throughout his nature. And behind much of his prose there is the assurance of such a general principle firmly held. In matters of education, for instance, Milton believed that the full treasury of learning, and not as of old a mere scholastic selection, should be open to the student. But there must be within that treasury a disciplined and graded choice. And the highest human faculty, that of right reason, must try to make that choice. Milton's essay *On Education* is such an attempt. Marriage must rest on the principle not of rigidly legalized but of congenial choice. Hence divorce of incompatible mates is right. The press must be allowed freedom, because without it a rationally disciplined choice is impossible.

It is when we come to matters of specifically religious discipline and liberty that Milton's emotions become most difficult to assess and to sort out.

A very important side of religious liberty had to do with the Scriptures, and it is one on which a modern is very apt to go wrong. The first instinct in a modern is to look on a belief in the inspiration and self-sufficiency of the Scriptures as a narrowing, not a liberating, doctrine; and that is a prime error. Even if some Protestants may have had secret thoughts in that sense, they could not at the beginning of the movement have seen the Scriptures that way round. On the contrary for them the Scriptures were a land till recently but imperfectly known, of extreme beauty and diversity, but spoilt by fences and prohibitory notices; a land better but less known than the regions that on all sides hemmed it in. David Ogg[1] notices as a prime innovation of the Reformation the desire to escape from the hampering peripheral matters to the lucid but wantonly obscured central ones:

> The 'gloss', or comment, is . . . eminently typical of later medievalism: the primary text, whether it be the Gospels or Justinian, is shrouded in a mass of commentary which may obscure or distort the original, and the scholar tended to surrender his common sense to the task of 'scripturiant margin-

[1] *The Reformation* (London, 1927), 3–4.

filling'. This process sacrificed clarity to subtlety: the result was that by the end of the fifteenth century there existed an enormous secondary literature, all based more or less on originals, but embodying many strained and unwarranted interpretations of doctrines originally expounded with a measure of brevity and lucidity. Indeed, intellectual subtlety was one of the later medieval virtues: it was, unfortunately, not confined to academic spheres, but extended to matters on which the humble believer might have hoped for clarity and guidance. Most of the great reformers reacted against this literature.

Calvin, in the prefatory chapter of his *Institutes*, put the clarity of Scripture against the sophistries with which it had been entangled, as one of his main arguments for writing:

All the Fathers with one heart execrated, and with one mouth protested against, contaminating the word of God with the subtleties of sophists, and involving it in the brawls of dialecticians. Do our adversaries keep within these limits when the sole occupation of their lives is to entwine and entangle the simplicity of Scripture with endless disputes and worse than sophistical jargon?

In the fourteenth chapter of his first book Calvin speaks of the angels and remarks how much plainer St Paul is than Dionysius the Areopagite with his complicated hierarchies. And yet St Paul *knew*, having been rapt into the third heaven. So we must disregard the nugatory wisdom of Dionysius and 'endeavour to ascertain from the simple doctrine of Scripture what it is the Lord's pleasure we should know concerning angels'. This plainness of Scripture removed it from the clutches of the specialist, that is the priestly theologian, and opened it to the interpretation of any sane and pious layman— a great new freedom. No wonder then that the confinement of necessary divine truth to the Scriptures was far outweighed in Protestant eyes by the accompanying liberty of choice and of interpretation within the confines. And about this liberty Protestants continued to feel passionately, up to and beyond Milton's day.

How did Milton feel on these matters? Not, I believe, in the same clear and whole-hearted and unencumbered way in which he felt about the *general* principle of discipline and liberty. On one point, indeed, he felt whole-heartedly, namely the right of individual interpretation and of individual immediate contact with God, unregulated by priestly mediation. On the individual's contact with God, as felt by Milton, I need not enlarge, in view of the section on Milton and Protestantism in my *Miltonic Setting*, but to the sustained ardour of his belief in the right of individual interpretation his last pamphlet, *Of True Religion*, bears eloquent witness. Here he goes so far as to argue tolerance of any sincere interpreter of Scripture, into whatever errors he may fall:

> It is a humane frailty to err, and no man is infallible here on earth. But so long as all these profess to set the Word of God only before them as the Rule of faith and obedience; and use all diligence and sincerity of heart, by reading, by learning, by study, by prayer, for illumination of the holy Spirit, to understand the Rule and obey it, they have done what man can do: God will assuredly pardon them, as he did the friends of *Job*, good and pious men, though much mistaken, as there it appears, in some Points of Doctrin.[1]

There you have Milton's true and unencumbered feeling for disciplined liberty. But over the premise that the Scriptures are inspired and self-sufficient his feelings were mixed. In suggesting such a mixture we must first take into account two things that go against it.

First, the contemporary suasion in favour of the unique inspiration of the canonical books was overwhelming; and it was not in the least a primarily Puritan matter. Of the Thirty-nine Articles of the Church of England the first five deal with the Trinity, and the sixth with the 'sufficiency of the holy Scriptures for salvation'. This is the text of the sixth article:

> Holy Scripture containeth all things necessary to salvation: so that whatsoever is not read therein, nor may be proved thereby, is not to be required of any man, that it should be believed as an article of the Faith, or be thought requisite or necessary to salvation. In the name of the holy Scripture we do understand

[1] vi, 168.

those Canonical Books of the Old and New Testament, of whose authority was never any doubt in the Church.

Ussher (1581–1656), Archbishop of Armagh and a central figure of Anglican orthodoxy, published two short catechisms, the *Principles of Christian Religion* and the *Method of the Doctrine of the Christian Religion*; and these speak of holy Scripture at once, before speaking of the nature of God. Here is the first of the two openings:[1]

> *Question:* What sure ground have we to build our Religion upon?
> *Answer:* The Word of God, contained in the Scriptures.
> *Question:* What are those Scriptures?
> *Answer:* Holy writings, indited by God himself for the perfect instruction of his Church.
> *Question:* What gather you of this, that God is the author of these writings?
> *Answer:* That therefore they are of most certain credit, and highest authority.
> *Question:* How serve they for the perfect instruction of the Church?
> *Answer:* In that they are able to instruct us sufficiently, in all points of faith that we are bound to believe, and all good duties that we are bound to practise.

Secondly, Milton never faltered in his professions of belief in the uniqueness and sufficiency of the Scriptures. It is patent in the early pamphlets; it is the foundation of the *De Doctrina Christiana*, as he explains in his preface:

> For my own part, I adhere to the holy Scriptures alone. . . . Any other judges or paramount interpreters of the Christian belief, together with all implicit faith as it is called, I, in common with the whole Protestant Church, refuse to recognize.

In *Paradise Lost*, the belief can occur but incidentally, yet occur it does. Michael, describing the world after the purity of primitive Christianity, tells Adam (xii, 508–514),

> Wolves shall succeed for teachers, grievous Wolves,
> Who all the sacred mysteries of Heav'n
> To thir own vile advantages shall turn

[1] Works, ed. C. R. Elrington (Dublin, 1864), xi, 181.

> Of lucre and ambition, and the truth
> With superstitions and traditions taint,
> Left only in those written Records pure,
> Though not but by the Spirit understood.

Finally, Milton's one pamphlet written late in life, *Of True Religion* (1673), has as its main theme the unique value of Scripture as a field of free interpretation and as the main weapon against popery.

It would seem therefore, initially, very unlikely that Milton could lack total emotional allegiance to the doctrine of scriptural sufficiency. And yet there are signs that he did, and those signs are all the more important in view of the immense pressure in the other direction. The thirtieth chapter of the first book of the *De Doctrina* is on the holy Scriptures. In it Milton first reasserts the principles laid down in his preface that 'the rule and canon of faith is Scripture alone. Scripture is the sole judge of controversies', and that 'every believer has a right to interpret the Scriptures for himself. . . . The expositions of the public interpreter can be of no use to him'. But then he goes on to say (as he hints also in the last line of the passage from *Paradise Lost*) that as well as external Scripture (the canonical books of the Bible) there is an internal Scripture, 'the Holy Spirit, written in the hearts of believers'. This internal Scripture is superior,

> for the external Scripture, or written word, particularly of the New Testament has been liable to frequent corruption, and in some instances has been corrupted, through the number and occasionally the bad faith of those by whom it has been handed down, the variety and discrepancy of the original manuscripts, and the additional diversity produced by subsequent transcripts and printed editions. But the Spirit which leads to truth cannot be corrupted, neither is it easy to deceive a man who is really spiritual.

Milton is puzzled by this fallibility in the divine word, for he adds:

> It is difficult to conjecture the purpose of Providence in committing the writings of the New Testament to such uncertain

and variable guardianship, unless it were to teach us by this very circumstance that the Spirit which is given to us is a more certain guide than Scripture.

A weakness of all early Protestant reliance on Scripture was the mixed motives that animated it. As well as the genuine thirst for the purity of God's word was the instinctive knowledge that for political purposes Scripture provided a rigid frame of authority with which to oppose the authority arrogated to itself by the Catholic Church. Even if the genuine thirst dwindled, the absolute authority of Scripture remained indispensable for political reasons. Milton was not exempt from such motives, as his last pamphlet clearly shows. But I cannot believe that such mixed motives left him quite happy emotionally. When it comes to the internal Scripture, Milton feels with all his nature. He is one with the Quaker doctrine of the inner light and with that of the Cambridge Platonists concerning the right reason; and wherever in *Paradise Lost* he invokes the Spirit he does so with full emotional conviction. But his words on scriptural corruption betray a doubt concerning a doctrine of Scripture whose very strength was a rigidity and a confinement not really congenial to the free working of the Spirit. It was a rigidity that led to a superstitious reverence for the canonical books and no others, with such a practice as opening the Bible and putting a finger on a verse at random to obtain guidance in doubt. Once you admit possibilities of faulty transmission you break a superstition that assumes the uniform and inviolable sacrosanctity of every syllable. But the main point is that the whole character of Milton's belief in the freedom to interpret is alien to a doctrine that segregates just these books and no others into a sacred class apart. If man's reason, aided by the Holy Spirit, can interpret the canonical scriptures, why can it not interpret other religious works? And if it can, this initial segregation becomes superfluous. Milton does not in fact argue thus, but it is hard to believe that, having made the division into internal and external Scripture, he did not at least dimly entertain such thoughts. To put it in another way, could the writer of *Areopagitica*, who believed in the individual's choice in the utmost range of good and evil, believe emotionally in any doctrine that authoritatively segregated certain writings as different from the rest, and exacted a preliminary obedience to them?

It is possible that this conflict in Milton's mind over Scripture—politics forcing him to accept scriptural sufficiency absolutely, his temperament finding it alien to him—explains the harshness of Christ's words on classical poetry in *Paradise Regained* (iv, 331–64).

Readers will never agree on the nature of the speech where these words occur. It is probable that every sentiment there can be abundantly substantiated in theological writings; and this for some readers will explain everything, will remove all difficulties. Others will insist that the tone matters more than the substance, that the fact of derivation matters less than the turn given to the things derived. The point will be that Christ speaks bitterly, and more bitterly than the context demanded:

> All our Law and Story strew'd
> With Hymns, our Psalms with artful terms inscrib'd,
> Our Hebrew Songs and Harps in *Babylon*,
> That pleas'd so well our Victors ear, declare
> That rather *Greece* from us these Arts deriv'd;
> Ill imitated, while they loudest sing
> The vices of thir Deities, and thir own
> In Fable, Hymn, or Song, so personating
> Thir Gods ridiculous, and themselves past shame.
> Remove their swelling Epithetes thick laid
> As varnish on a Harlots cheek, the rest,
> Thin sown with aught of profit or delight,
> Will far be found unworthy to compare
> With *Sion's* songs, to all true tasts excelling.

Milton had already written about the superiority of Hebrew to Greek lyric, but in how different a tone. In the preface to the second book of *Reason of Church Government* he had mentioned as possible objects of poetic imitation

those magnific Odes and Hymns wherein Pindarus and Callimachus are in most things worthy, some others in their frame judicious, in their matter most an end faulty: But those frequent songs throughout the law and prophets beyond all these, not in their divine argument alone, but in the very critical art of composition may be easily made appear over all the kinds of Lyric poesy, to be incomparable.

Why should Milton say the same thing here without rancour and in *Paradise Regained* so bitterly? It may be answered that Milton speaking in cool prose and Milton's Christ repelling the tempter cannot be expected to speak alike. Yet Christ would have answered Satan quite as effectively without the bitterness; indeed more effectively because with less exaggeration. And those who see in Christ's bitterness the sign of a conflict in Milton himself do not lack some evidence. And if it is a case of conflict, that conflict may have to do with the status of Scripture, for the comparison is between the uninspired lyrics of Greece and the inspired lyrics in some of the canonical books.

The other matter of liberty in which Milton's emotions are involved in a more complicated way is that specifically Christian liberty which could be attained when the sinner, born to sin, had been redeemed by Christ and adopted by God, being made free of the bondage and incrimination of the Old Law. But this conception of liberty cannot be separated from the theological scheme to which it belongs and it brings me to the most difficult of all the questions posed in this essay: Milton's emotional response, as revealed in his poetry, to the central things of Protestant theology.

To some version of the orthodox scheme of innocence, the Fall, original sin, and redemption through Christ, Milton paid complete emotional allegiance. Nor was that allegiance compromised because he was not greatly concerned with the approach to God *per imitationem Christi*, because his Christ is hardly at all the Jesus of the Gospels and mainly the Pauline Redeemer (the Christ of *Paradise Regained* having little resemblance to the Jesus who in the Synoptic Gospels, after baptism, was tempted in the wilderness). But how central to his emotions was the idea of redemption through Christ, should have been made clear in my section on the *Crisis of*

154

Paradise Lost. In writing of the redemption of Adam and Eve in Book Ten, Milton was much less tied to the details of Puritan orthodoxy than when in Book Three he makes God explain his intentions or when in Book Twelve he describes redemption after the Law has led man into a still deeper incrimination. And it remains to be considered how Milton was likely to be tied to that orthodoxy and what was the emotional effect of that bond.

Milton grew up in a Puritan family, whose parish priest was Richard Stock, a Puritan, bred at St John's, Cambridge, when William Perkins, the great English Calvinist preacher, was at the height of his influence in that university. When Milton read Calvin we do not know,[1] but we can be certain that he was open to that body of Calvinist doctrine to which Calvin had supplied the emotional as well as the intellectual ingredient. One reason why Calvinism was so strong is that it gave a special and highly dramatic form to more general Protestant doctrine. Of this there is an excellent account in William Haller's *Rise of Puritanism.*[2] Protestantism itself was less new than selective, and it drew strength from being more simple than the old religion as it was before the Jesuits and the Council of Trent. Puritanism gained further strength by concentrating fiercely on certain phases of Christian doctrine; and the resulting frame of belief was briefly the following.

In traditional theology the two main ways of access to God were through the contemplation of natural things (*per speculum creaturarum* as mentioned before) and through the imitation of Christ. The Puritans did not deny these ways but they were more interested in another main matter of orthodox theology: the dogma derived from certain chapters of St Paul, especially the eighth of *Romans.* From this dogma they elaborated a regular drama of salvation, which was their living mythology. The drama began with God's creation of mankind from nothing and proceeded to the utter depravity of man through the

---

[1] But we do know that in 1641 he was prepared to be critical of Calvin. He said to his opponent in *Animadversions* (iii, 149), 'You think then you are fairly quit of this proofe, because *Calvin* interprets it for you, as if we could be put off with *Calvins* name, unless we be convinc't with *Calvins* reason.'

[2] New York, 1938, chaps. iii and iv.

disobedience of Adam and through man's subsequent failure to follow God's will as declared in his law. In this process Satan was of prime importance, since it was he who defeated Adam, the Old Man, in the Garden. The process was reversed by Christ, the New Man, and principally when he defeated Satan in the Wilderness. Out of depraved humanity God by his grace chose out certain favoured people, the rest being left for damnation. Through the victorious act of Christ these became more numerous than under the old dispensation. And there was the prospect of Christ and his Saints triumphing on earth. The holy life was precisely mapped out in the stages of election, vocation, justification, sanctification, glorification; and Puritans developed a novel interest in the minute details of their souls' health. But though elected and called and so on, the Saint was never free from sin. He was a fighting not an innocent soul. And though he was sure of salvation if he persisted in his fight, he knew, with Bunyan, that there was a gateway to Hell even at the foot of the heavenly mountain. So he must wear the whole armour of God as detailed by St Paul and never relax in his fight against Satan. But though the Saint was not innocent, he was no longer a slave to the Old Law; he enjoyed a new liberty as the adopted son of God, and his efforts, though imperfect, were nevertheless acceptable.

From this account it is plain that Puritanism was a religion of hope as well as of despair. There was the hope that God would choose you and the hope that one day a holy community would be founded on earth. And this second hope may have helped on the faint beginnings of the idea of human progress in the seventeenth century. More important, it gave the Puritan a motive, something to fight for. Equally important, the Puritan myth made for human equality. The doctrine of utter depravity was a great leveller, reducing all men to such abjectness that there was nothing to choose between them. And when it came to election, God's choice was arbitrary and quite unsnobbish. It was also a direct choice, with the consequent superfluity of any human medium.

This Protestant drama, largely the creation of Calvin, was

powerful because it combined logic with emotion. At its root was the emotional apprehension of omnipotence. And that apprehension could be satisfied only by divesting mankind of every shred of power and virtue. Calvin in the preface to his *Institutes* puts this position with passion:

> What accords better and more aptly with faith than to acknowledge ourselves divested of all virtue that we may be clothed by God, devoid of all goodness that we may be filled by him, the slaves of sin that he may give us freedom, blind that he may enlighten, lame that he may cure, and feeble that he may sustain us; to strip ourselves of all ground of glorying that he alone may shine forth glorious, and we be glorified in him? When these things are said by us, our adversaries interpose and complain that in this way we overturn some blind light of nature, fancied preparatives, free will, and works meritorious of eternal salvation, with their own supererogations also; because they cannot bear that the entire praise and glory of all goodness, virtue, justice, and wisdom, should remain with God.

Calvin does not flinch from the consequences of his initial assumption. He is horror-struck by the heresy that God made mankind from himself and not from nothing (*Institutes*, i, chap. 15). Any dignity acquired by man through being made from the divine essence would only be so much detraction from the divine majesty. After the Fall man must be utterly depraved because 'man cannot arrogate anything, however minute, to himself without robbing God of his honour' (ii, chap. 2). And again Calvin's sense of man's depravity is passionate:

> The mind of man is so entirely alienated from the righteousness of God that he cannot conceive, desire, or design anything but what is wicked, distorted, impure, and iniquitous; that his heart is so thoroughly envenomed by sin, that it can breathe out nothing but corruption and rottenness; that if some men occasionally make a show of goodness, their mind is ever interwoven with hypocrisy and deceit, their soul inwardly bound with the fetters of wickedness. (ii, chap. 5.)

As man's nature is devoid of all virtue, so must his will be deprived of all power, for to allow fallen man the option of making any motion on his own part back towards God would rob God of his supreme credit in manifesting an act of grace. If God is under the least obligation to pity man, if any kindness to him is not an act of absolutely arbitrary will, his glory would suffer. In the same way, if God's grace did not operate directly on the recipient, if in particular it ever passed through a human mediator, his glory would suffer. And that doctrine was the great weapon against the elaborate system of mediation devised by the Catholic Church. But, in this world, besides the direct communication of God to his elect, some further guide was wanted. It had to be divine, and it was found in Scripture, the dictated word of God.

It is most remarkable that in spite of Milton's Puritan home and his Puritan tutor there, Thomas Young ('his school master was a puritan in Essex, who cutt his haire short'), his early writings show no signs of being influenced by some of the very root matters of the Puritan creed. In *Upon the Circumcision* and *At a Solemn Music*, where he could have done so, Milton drops no hint of any inclination to the doctrine of utter depravity. In the *Prolusions* Platonism and the bounty of God's creation are the dominant religious themes. In the *Second Prolusion*, on the harmony of the spheres, it is of course natural that he should treat a Platonic subject Platonically, but he also refers obliquely to sin and the Fall and could, had he wished, have insinuated some Calvinism. But he is far from doing so. After saying, in terms of classical mythology, that fallen man can no longer hear the heavenly music, he goes on:

for how can we become sensitive to this heavenly sound while our souls are, as Persius says, bowed to the ground and lacking in every heavenly element? But if our souls were pure, chaste, and white as snow, as was Pythagoras's of old, then indeed our ears would ring and be filled with that exquisite music of the stars in their orbits.[1]

And still more Platonic is Milton's account of man's relation to his creator in the *Seventh Prolusion*:

[1] *Private Correspondence and Academic Exercises*, ed. P. B. Tillyard, 67.

It is a belief familiar and generally accepted that the great Creator of the world, while constituting all else fleeting and perishable, infused into man, besides what was mortal, a certain divine spirit, a part of himself as it were, which is immortal, imperishable, and exempt from death and extinction. After wandering about upon the earth for some time, like some heavenly visitant, in holiness and righteousness, this spirit was to take its flight upward to the heaven whence it had come and to return to its abode and home which was its birthright.[1]

Milton then says that the natural food of this divine element in man is contemplation and that a prime object of contemplation are God's wonderful works:

Survey from every angle the entire aspect of these things and you will perceive that the great artificer of this mighty fabric established it for his own glory. The more deeply we delve into the wondrous wisdom, the marvellous skill, and the astounding variety of its creation, the greater grow the wonder and awe we feel for its creator.[2]

Here, far from insinuating any Puritan theology, Milton resorts to the traditional theology of the glories of creation. In *Comus*, the Brothers and the Lady are indeed chosen spirits, and the Lady has to rely on the immediate help of heaven, but there is no hint of their election on the Calvinist scheme or of their utter depravity before it. And yet from his early prose works it appears that Milton had been at least a nominal Calvinist. This (and simultaneously a hint of his forthcoming break with a main Calvinist tenet) appears in the third chapter of the second book of the *Doctrine and Discipline of Divorce*. There he speaks of the 'Jesuits', and 'that sect among us which is nam'd *Arminius*' as from the other camp, and of 'those minds which perhaps out of a vigilant and wary conscience except against predestination'. In *Areopagitica* very shortly after he himself 'excepted against predestination' and later he went against the very core of Calvinism by arguing that God created the world from himself, and that the Fall did not extinguish all traces of man's original virtue.

[1] Ibid., 107.
[2] Ibid., 108.

But though Milton seems to owe little to Calvin in the relation of creature to creator, he does owe something to the Puritan way of thinking about Christ's redeeming work and Christian liberty. It is of course very hard to be sure that one is right in mentioning Calvin or Perkins or some other Puritan divine rather than St Paul or St Augustine in speaking of whence Milton derived his version of central Christian dogma. Nevertheless, the extreme emphasis which Milton puts on the legalistic side of redemption and on Christian Liberty does seem to ally him with the Calvinists. It also has an immediate bearing on the subject of this essay, because it is the poetical passages dealing with those matters that have given most offence to readers and about whose emotional character there remains the greatest doubt: I mean the celestial colloquy in *Paradise Lost*, iii, 80–343, and Michael's account of the Law and man's freedom from it through Christ's redemption in xii, 285–465. It is not, I believe, an accident that the one piece of dogmatic theology that occurs amidst the rich mythology in the hymn of the *Nativity Ode* concerns the redemption:

> But wisest Fate sayes no,
> This must not yet be so,
> The Babe lies yet in smiling Infancy,
> That on the bitter cross
> Must redeem our loss:

and largely because the doctrine, in greater and in legalistic detail, reappears in a poem written a little later, *Upon the Circumcision*.

> Alas, how soon our sin
> Sore doth begin
> His Infancy to sease!
> O more exceeding love or law more just?
> Just law indeed, but more exceeding love!
> For we by rightfull doom remediles
> Were lost in death, till he that dwelt above
> High thron'd in secret bliss, for us frail dust
> Emptied his glory, ev'n to nakedness;

And that great Cov'nant which we still transgress
Intirely satisfied,
And the full wrath beside
Of vengeful Justice bore for our excess.

There is a genuine emotional kinship between *Intirely satisfi'd . . . full wrath* in this poem and the tremendous line, *The rigid satisfaction, death for death*, in the third book of *Paradise Lost*. We have to do with an early and persistent element in Milton's emotions. Can we define this element as it comes out in the poetry?

Plainly this is hard. On the other hand it is not so hard today as it was earlier in the century when Rousseauish doctrines about the nature of man prevailed and the doctrine of original sin was relegated to a restricted orthodoxy. One of the most important recent changes of mind in the general, unorthodox public is a new willingness to accept in some form the doctrine of original sin and of the need for some kind of regeneration. That is some help, but we must in compensation remember that not only unorthodox but most orthodox opinion does not accept, save in an allegorical way, the basis of the Christian scheme in the incrimination of Adam. The natural impulse in most readers who are prepared to consider Milton's theology seriously at all is to make him quite sincere and unimpeded in his general acceptance of the Christian scheme and to detect signs of conflict when his feelings encounter the rigid Puritan statement of it. In such an impulse there is very patently the danger of creating the object of criticism in the critic's image. Though recognizing the danger, I believe the impulse to point to some elements of the truth. And now I turn to the most relevant passages in Milton's poetry.

Although the lines *Upon the Circumcision* show what a deep hold the rigid doctrine of redemption had on the youthful Milton they do not betray any strain in the act of acceptance. And it is just because the two passages in *Paradise Lost* differ so much in their tone that one suspects the possibility of strain in them. Nor is a change of feeling in the interval unlikely. It was between the writing of the *Doctrine and Dis-*

cipline of Divorce and *Areopagitica* that Milton forsook Calvin for Arminius over the question of predestination. Is it not also true that *Areopagitica* is warm-hearted and abundant in feeling and the very reverse of precise and legalistic?

> How great a vertue is temperance, how much of moment through the whole life of man! Yet God commits the managing so great a trust, without particular Law or prescription, wholly to the demeanour of every grown man. And therefore when he himself tabl'd the Jews from heaven, that Omer which was every man's daily portion of Manna, is computed to have bin more than might have well suffic'd the heartiest feeder thrice as many meals.[1]

Surely this is the true Milton speaking, the possessor of a passionate and superabundant, not a tidy, mind. Is it not therefore possible that Milton came to be uneasy about the form in which he had received the doctrine of the Redemption and yet was unable to get away from it, so powerfully had it been stamped into his mind in boyhood?

The two relevant passages in *Paradise Lost* (iii, 80–343 and xii, 285–465) deal with the same theological matters, and the first suffers from complications absent from the second. It is a mixture of sublime poetry and of passages that offend or chill many readers. Much of the offence may be due to God's speaking in person. It is somehow inappropriate, except in the simplicity of a Miracle Play, for God to have to explain and justify his own decrees. The risk here therefore of wrongly psychologizing on what may be a mere mistake of technique is too big to be run. On the other hand it is perfectly appropriate that, as happens in the second passage, an archangel should instruct the first man in the ways of God. What can be said then about Michael's account of the Redemption? To Adam's question about the fight between Christ and Satan, Michael replies (xii, 386–419):

> Dream not of thir fight,
> As of a Duel, or the local wounds
> Of head or heel: not therefore joynes the Son
> Manhood to God-head, with more strength to foil

[1] iv, 309–10.

Thy enemie; nor so is overcome
Satan, whose fall from Heav'n, a deadlier bruise,
Disabl'd not to give thee thy deaths wound:
Which he, who comes thy Saviour, shall recure,
Not by destroying *Satan*, but his works
In thee and in thy Seed; nor can this be,
But by fulfilling that which thou didst want,
Obedience to the Law of God, impos'd
On penaltie of death, and suffering death,
The penaltie to thy transgression due,
And due to theirs which out of thine will grow:
So onely can high Justice rest appaid.
The Law of God exact he shall fulfill,
Both by obedience and by love, though love
Alone fulfill the Law; thy punishment
He shall endure by coming in the Flesh
To a reproachful life and cursed death,
Proclaiming Life to all who shall believe
In his redemption, and that his obedience
Imputed becomes theirs by Faith, his merits
To save them, not their own, though legal works.
For this he shall live hated, be blasphem'd,
Seis'd on by force, judg'd, and to death condemnd
A shameful and accurst, naild to the Cross
By his own Nation, slaine for bringing Life;
But to the Cross he nailes thy Enemies,
The Law that is against thee, and the sins
Of all mankinde, with him there crucifi'd,
Never to hurt them more who rightly trust
In this his satisfaction.

In my *Milton* I noted a certain lack of feeling in this account
of the crucifixion and cited a passage from Traherne in contrast. That citation was not apt, for it expressed a type of
feeling outside that Puritan myth to which in this passage
Milton was certainly loyal. What is surprising is that he recounts this, the culminating scene in the great Puritan drama,
with so comparatively little energy and passion. As passionate
writing, the lines on Christian liberty a little before and the
lines on the world's decay a little after quite overshadow the
account of Redemption. On the other hand Milton insists, with

an emphasis he could have avoided had he wished, on the legalism of the transaction. Had not Milton written more passionately in nearby places, it could be argued that he was for some reason tired.[1] Ingenuity could find many explanations, but a possible one is that Milton was powerless either to free himself from, or to impassion, the legalism that then for all Christians, but especially for the Puritans, was inseparable from the doctrine of the Redemption.

Linked with the doctrine of the Redemption was that of Christian Liberty. Man, saved by Christ's redeeming power from his own sin and his subsequent bondage to the Law, could be adopted into the sonship of God, re-inheriting his self-lost birthright. As God's son, man gives free service to God; and that is true liberty. Moreover the service given is different from the service exacted, but impossible of performance, under the Law. Calvin in his chapter on Christian Liberty in the third book of the *Institutes* asserts that man's position under the Law was that of a slave. Only the complete performance of every duty fulfils the obligations of a slave; only so can the slave face his master. But sons stand in a relation to their father which allows merit to imperfect or even faulty work. I should say that Milton accepted early in life, and maintained throughout it strong and unimpaired, this sense of filial relation of man and God. It appears in the bold virtue of the Brothers and the Lady in *Comus*, and in *Samson Agonistes* where Samson first feels the loss of and finally regains the filial position. In between it appears in the pamphlets, in such a phrase as 'filial and adoptive boldness' towards God, and very eminently in *Paradise Lost*. As soon as Adam and Eve appear, Milton tells us of their filial relation to God (iv, 288–94).

> Two of far nobler shape erect and tall,
> Godlike erect, with native Honour clad
> In naked Majestie seemd Lords of all,
> And worthie seemd, for in thir looks Divine

[1] C. S. Lewis (125) considers the whole of books xi and xii (except the very end and some fine moments) to fall off greatly. I do not agree about book xi and I think he is but partially right over book xii.

> The image of thir glorious Maker shon,
> Truth, Wisdome, Sanctitude severe and pure,
> Severe, but in true filial freedom plac't.

The great instance of filial freedom in action is Adam's conversation with God about his need for a consort in Book Eight with its sublime conclusion (452-7):

> Hee ended, or I heard no more, for now
> My earthly by his Heav'nly overpowerd,
> Which it had long stood under, streind to the highth
> In that celestial Colloquie sublime,
> As with an object that excels the sense,
> Dazl'd and spent, sunk down.

And Milton's definitive exposition of the doctrine as applied to fallen man is put in Michael's mouth in the twelfth book (285-306):

> To whom thus *Michael.* Doubt not but that sin
> Will reign among them, as of thee begot;
> And therefore was Law given them to evince
> Thir natural pravitie, by stirring up
> Sin against Law to fight; that when they see
> Law can discover sin, but not remove,
> Save by those shadowie expiations weak,
> The blood of Bulls and Goats, they may conclude
> Some blood more precious must be paid for Man,
> Just for unjust, that in such righteousness
> To them by Faith imputed, they may finde
> Justification towards God, and peace
> Of Conscience, which the Law by Ceremonies
> Cannot appease, nor Man the moral part
> Perform, and not performing cannot live.
> So Law appears imperfet, and but giv'n
> With purpose to resign them in full time
> Up to a better Cov'nant, disciplin'd
> From shadowie Types to Truth, from Flesh to Spirit,
> From imposition of strict Laws, to free
> Acceptance of large Grace, from servil fear
> To filial, works of Laws to works of Faith.

Rajan, who has written better than most critics on the two

last books of *Paradise Lost*, characterizes these lines by 'the massive and moving finality' with which they sum up the relationship of the Gospel to the Law:

> Every phrase, every word almost, says more completely and more nobly what a hundred other writers have said before. Yet even those who can neither recover nor respond to this network of allusion can surely appreciate the severe yet ardent splendour of those antitheses, the upsurge of joyousness that moves in Milton's mind when he celebrates the union of discipline with freedom.[1]

That is truly said; and the legalistic side of the doctrine is successfully fused with the ardour with which Milton describes the state of filial liberty. The doctrine of filial liberty was one which Milton not only absorbed from his Puritan upbringing but felt in his blood.

But if Milton was highly selective in the emotional allegiance he gave to the more dogmatic sides of the Puritan myth, he was whole-hearted in his initial allegiance to the more practical sides. Naturally ardent and active, he found the Puritan ideal of the wayfaring or warfaring Christian entirely congenial. This has long been a familiar matter, and there is no need to dwell on it here. But it is worth mentioning a side of it that William Haller[2] has recently brought to the light. The typical field of the Puritan Christian warfare was the pulpit. Milton was born into the last great phase of Puritan preaching in the Anglican church; and his parents, seeing his talents, thought of him as in that succession. But by the time he went to college the phase had passed, Laud had curbed militant Puritanism, and Milton, seeing how things were going, abandoned the idea of orders and conceived a hostility to the episcopacy that had caused things to be so. His poetry was the substitute for the other didacticism.

Milton's enthusiasm for the great practical hope of the Puritans, the establishment of a holy society in his own England, is again too well known to need comment. Much has been done recently to place Milton's part in the general move-

[1] 90–1.

[2] *The Rise of Puritanism*, Chapter vii.

ment, but that he did play this part is a matter of ancient knowledge. The holy society does not get into Milton's verse, though his early prose is full of it; but it is likely that the Round Table in his never written *Arthuriad* would have typified it.

It will never be clearly settled how far Milton's disillusionment over his country and its failure to seize its God-given chance has entered *Paradise Lost*. In particular what do the terrible lines near the end of the poem describing the course of the world after the growth of Popery denote?

> Truth shall retire
> Bestruck with slandrous darts, and works of Faith
> Rarely be found: so shall the World goe on,
> To good malignant, to bad men benigne,
> Under her own waight groaning, till the day
> Appeer of respiration to the just,
> And vengeance to the wicked. (535–41.)

Is the feeling here the bitter disillusion Milton himself lived through or mere acquiescence in a general pessimism about human affairs which in the Puritan tradition coexisted with the hope of a holy society duplicating at least temporarily the holiness of the primitive church? Here is a typical piece of pessimism from Calvin himself:

Human affairs have scarcely ever been so happily constituted as that the better course pleased the greater number. Hence the private vices of the multitude have generally resulted in public error, or rather that common consent in vice which these worthy men would have to be law. Any one with eyes may perceive that it is not one flood of evils which has deluged us; that many fatal plagues have invaded the globe; that all things rush headlong; so that either the affairs of men must be altogether despaired of, or we must not only resist but boldly attack prevailing evils.[1]

It is probable that there are both ingredients in the passage from *Paradise Lost* and that Milton used a Puritan way of thinking through which to express his own sense of the human tragedy.

[1] *Institutes*. Preface.

In writing on some of the religious matters about which Milton had mixed feelings I do not wish to suggest that this mixture was anything but exceptional. It counts for far less than the single-minded convictions and enthusiasms I described at the beginning of this section and in the section on the *Crisis of Paradise Lost*. Thus, in ending, I ask the reader to let his mind come to rest in the things that Milton asserts with such unhesitating passion in the culminating books of his epic.

Milton and Statius

ONE of the most strikingly neo-classic passages in Milton is the description in *Paradise Lost* of how Adam, awaiting Eve's return from her solitary horticulture and then learning her beguilement by the serpent, is frozen with horror and drops the garland he has woven for her. Here are the lines:

> Thus *Eve* with Countnance blithe her storie told;
> But in her Cheek distemper flushing glowd.
> On th' other side, *Adam*, soon as he heard
> The fatal Trespass done by *Eve*, amaz'd,
> Astonied stood and Blank, while horror chill
> Ran through his veins, and all his joynts relax'd;
> From his slack hand the Garland wreath'd for *Eve*
> Down drop'd, and all the faded Roses shed.

It is a description at once highly alive and highly mannered and conventional. The roses fade instantaneously in sympathy with the depression of Adam's spirit: their ruin is thrilling, and yet how extreme an example of the 'pathetic fallacy'! The whole picture reminds one immediately of the carefully staged compositions of Poussin; and Mario Praz might well have cited Milton's lines in his fine article.[1] We are somehow forced to picture the figures of Adam and Eve as Poussin would have painted them: noble, long-limbed, and with classical profiles.

Now if Milton's picture is so strongly neo-classic, we may expect classical prototypes. The astonishment of Adam is of course a simple reminiscence of conventional epic terror:

> Obstupuere animi, gelidusque per ima cucurrit
> ossa tremor.

[1] *Milton and Poussin* in *Seventeenth Century Studies presented to Sir Herbert Grierson* (Oxford 1938), 192–210.

But what of Adam's dropping the garland? The analogies cited in Todd's *Variorum Milton* from Propertius, Persius, and Spenser are remote and unconvincing. I suggest that Milton had at the back of his mind, whether consciously or not, some lines from one of the finest passages of Statius's *Thebaid* (vii, 148–50). Jupiter has just ordered Mars to incite the dallying troops of Adrastus to get on with their Theban expedition. Mars stages an alarm, and the troops hurriedly arm and begin to advance. Bacchus, protector of Thebes, receives a violent shock at the sight—

> purpureum tristi turbatus pectore vultum:
> non crines non serta loco, dextramque reliquit
> thyrsus, et intactae ceciderunt cornibus uvae.

Though it is the thyrsus that drops from Bacchus's hand, there are *garlands* too; while the grapes that fall from his horned head are *unimpaired* and as such could well have suggested the opposite condition of Adam's roses. There are rhythmical resemblances too. There is a heavy emphasis on the first syllables of both last lines followed by a heavy pause; emphasis and pause expressing the fall of the objects and their coming to rest. And when the verse is picked up again it persists only for a few feet to the end of the lines. The more melodramatic quality of Statius's lines in no way diminishes the probability of the loan. What Milton borrowed he always made his own.

APPENDIX B

Milton and Philostratus

THE description of how Sin and Death, strengthened by
the Fall of Man, threw a bridge over Chaos from Hell-
gate to the entrance of the universe is one of the grandest and
most elaborate in *Paradise Lost*. Not only is Milton's peculiar
power of creating visions, at once vivid and vast, at its height,
but the references to travel and literature, which came
naturally to Milton when his imagination was kindled, are
extremely rich.

We may expect unconscious recollections of the books he
had read. After the passage quoted in the text (p. 32)
Milton compares the causeway to the bridge built by Xerxes
over the Hellespont. But that was a wooden bridge; and I
fancy that it was another and more original structure that
Milton, perhaps with no conscious reminiscence, had in mind.
Philostratus in his life of Apollonius (I, 25) described the
tunnel a Babylonian Queen constructed under the Euphrates
to connect the palaces standing on different sides of that river.
Philostratus talks of

ἀπόρρητος γέφυρα, τὰ βασίλεια τὰ ἐπὶ ταῖς ὄχθαις ἀφανῶς ξυνάπτουσα. γυνὴ
γὰρ λέγεται Μηδεία τῶν ἐκείνη ποτὲ ἄρχουσα τὸν ποταμὸν ὑποζεῦξαι τρόπον ὃν
μήπω τις ποταμὸς ἐζεύχθη· λίθους γὰρ δὴ καὶ χαλκὸν καὶ ἄσφαλτον καὶ ὁπόσα
ἐς ἔφυδρον ξύνδεσιν ἀνθρώποις εὕρηται παρὰ τὰς ὄχθας τοῦ ποταμοῦ νήσασα, τὸ
ῥεῦμα ἐς λίμνας ἔτρεψε, ξηρόν τε ἤδη τὸν ποταμὸν ὤρυγεν ὀργυιὰς ἐς δύο σήραγγα
ἐργαζομένη κοίλην, ἵν' ἐς τὰ βασίλεια τὰ παρὰ ταῖς ὄχθαις ὥσπερ ἐκ γῆς ἀναφαίνοιτο,
καὶ ἤρεψεν αὐτὴν ἴσως τῷ τοῦ ῥεύματος δαπέδῳ. οἱ μὲν δὴ θεμέλιοι ἐβεβήκεσαν
καὶ οἱ τοῖχοι τῆς σήραγγος, ἅτε δὲ τῆς 'ασφάλτου δεομένης τοῦ ὕδατος ἐς τὸ λιθοῦσθαί
τε καὶ πήγνυσθαι ὁ Εὐφράτης ἐπαφείθη ὑγρῷ τῷ ὀρόφῳ καὶ ὧδε ἔστη τὸ ζεῦγμα.[1]

[1] 'A mysterious passage that invisibly connects the palaces on the banks. The
story goes that a queen named Medea spanned this river as never yet river was
spanned. She collected all the known materials for a water-tight revetment,
stone, and bronze, and bitumen, and what not, beside the banks, and then
diverted the stream. Next she excavated the dry river-bed to a depth of two
fathoms, making a hollow tunnel which should issue in an access to the river-
side palaces just as if no river were there; and roofed it level with the river-
bottom. Lastly, when the foundations and side-walls of the tunnel were in place,
and the bitumen only needed water in order to petrify and stiffen, the stream
was let in upon the roof while it was still soft, and thus the passage was made.'
(J. S. Phillimore's translation.)

171

There is of course a difference between the two structures: one was a causeway, the other a subway. But both were unique, and in Milton's mind Babylon would be connected with the powers of Hell. There are some striking resemblances. The makers of both bridges began by piling heaps of varied material. Verbally there is nothing so striking in Milton's passage as the 'Mace petrific' and the '*Asphaltic* slime'. In Philostratus we find λίθους and ἄσφαλτον close together and again ἄσφαλτον followed by λιθοῦσθαι.

No more than a probability can be established. I cannot recall any Miltonic reference to Philostratus. But if Burton was the channel through which Keats derived the plot of *Lamia* from Philostratus, Milton had probably read Philostratus too. And if he had read him, this striking description could hardly have fallen out of so retentive a memory.

Index

173